SAGE was founded in 1965 by Sara Miller McCune to support the dissemination of usable knowledge by publishing innovative and high-quality research and teaching content. Today, we publish over 900 journals, including those of more than 400 learned societies, more than 800 new books per year, and a growing range of library products including archives, data, case studies, reports, and video. SAGE remains majority-owned by our founder, and after Sara's lifetime will become owned by a charitable trust that secures our continued independence.

Los Angeles | London | New Delhi | Singapore | Washington DC | Melbourne

Advance Praise

This is the book every millennial needs to read! Utkarsh's engaging storytelling provides a roadmap for what it means to 'find your passion' and other misconceptions of the business world. Insightful and practical—you won't be able to put it down!

Marshall Goldsmith, New York Times *#1 bestselling author of* Triggers, Mojo, *and* What Got You Here Won't Get You There

As the creator of the term FOMO, I loved how Utkarsh explored its nuances and offered tangible principles for shaping meaningful careers. The case studies in *The Seductive Illusion of Hard Work* are powerful—from the cognitive biases of the creator of Sherlock Holmes to the quirks of Paul Erdos, the legendary mathematician and networker. Given its cross-cultural and multi-generational appeal, I recommend it to anyone interested in understanding the future of work.

Patrick McGinnisis, *Creator of the term FOMO and leading Venture Capitalist*

Utkarsh's book is an uniquely interesting take on career intelligence and the future of work. It is sprinkled with original insights and relatable stories that will resonate not only with millennials but also with senior executives and founders.

Pramath Raj Sinha, *Founder of Ashoka University, Harappa Education*

This book is a fascinating collection of mental models and career principles for discovering one's purpose. Utkarsh is a powerful storyteller whose narratives cause us to rethink how to work effectively.

Tarun Khanna, *Jorge Paulo Lemann Professor, Harvard Business School*

Utkarsh has a very interesting and sometimes counterintuitive take on the paths to success in life. This book is a very practical guide with tips that will make you rethink many things that you assumed or took for granted, especially your definition of success.

Sri Rajan, *Partner in Bain & Company, San Francisco, US*

This book hits so many sweet spots: It is broad (containing examples from science, arts, sports and, of course, business) but deep; it is academic yet actionable; it offers complex ideas but in bite-sized, readable, simple prose. One reason for this is Utkarsh Amitabh's career achievements, which span mainstream career success, entrepreneurial achievement and academic knowledge. The book contains none of the self-promotional clichés typical of business successes—he speaks as a trusted advisor who has the authority, experience and compassion to be the voice of his generation.

Tanya Menon, *Organizational Psychologist and TED Speaker*

Community, collaboration and courage are timeless. In the new world we live, these three defining themes will determine how we relook at work and life itself. Utkarsh has captured beautifully how these will work together and their interplay. An important book. An essential read.

Farzana Haque, *Patron, The Lincoln Center for the Performing Arts and The Juilliard School; Global Head for Strategic Group Accounts, TCS*

THE Seductive ILLUSION OF HARD WORK

THE *Seductive* ILLUSION OF HARD WORK

UTKARSH AMITABH

Los Angeles | London | New Delhi
Singapore | Washington DC | Melbourne

First published in 2020 by

SAGE Publications India Pvt. Ltd
B1/I-1 Mohan Cooperative Industrial Area
Mathura Road, New Delhi 110 044, India
www.sagepub.in

SAGE Publications Inc
2455 Teller Road
Thousand Oaks, California 91320, USA

SAGE Publications Ltd
1 Oliver's Yard, 55 City Road
London EC1Y 1SP, United Kingdom

SAGE Publications Asia-Pacific Pte Ltd
18 Cross Street #10-10/11/12
China Square Central
Singapore 048423

Published by Vivek Mehra for SAGE Publications India Pvt. Ltd. Typeset in 11/14.25 pt Adobe Caslon Pro by Fidus Design Pvt. Ltd, Chandigarh.

Library of Congress Control Number: 2020942657

ISBN: 978-93-5388-525-0 (PB)

SAGE Team: Neha Pal, Shruti Gupta, Aanchal Jain and Rajinder Kaur

I dedicate this book to
the Network Capital community
members and to everyone who has ever
received well meaning, yet misleading,
career advice along the lines of 'Follow
your passion' or 'Be yourself'. Although these
catchy phrases are meant to inspire, they often
end up confusing and adding anxiety to the
already perplexed millennial mind. This book
is an attempt to explore the origin of such
misconceptions and provide mental
models that help every person on the
planet augment his or her
career intelligence.

Thank you for choosing a SAGE product!
If you have any comment, observation or feedback,
I would like to personally hear from you.

Please write to me at **contactceo@sagepub.in**

Vivek Mehra, Managing Director and CEO, SAGE India.

Bulk Sales

SAGE India offers special discounts
for purchase of books in bulk.
We also make available special imprints
and excerpts from our books on demand.

For orders and enquiries, write to us at

Marketing Department
SAGE Publications India Pvt Ltd
B1/I-1, Mohan Cooperative Industrial Area
Mathura Road, Post Bag 7
New Delhi 110044, India

E-mail us at **marketing@sagepub.in**

Subscribe to our mailing list
Write to **marketing@sagepub.in**

This book is also available as an e-book.

Contents

Foreword

Previous industrial revolutions liberated humankind from animal power, made mass production possible and brought digital capabilities to billions of people. This fourth Industrial Revolution represents a fundamental change in the way we live, work and relate to one another. It is even challenging ideas about what it means to be human. The new revolution can be considered a new chapter in human development, as it is enabled by technology advances that are commensurate with those of the first, second and third Industrial Revolutions, and which are merging the physical, digital and biological worlds in ways that create both promise and peril.

Utkarsh's book talks about the power of communities to shape the future of work. Through clear examples and case studies, he is able to demonstrate how millennials can embrace the benefits of the fourth Industrial Revolution equitably and sustainably. I appreciated the fact that he makes it clear that the future of work not only entails the creation of new jobs but also figuring out how to augment human intelligence with new tools of technology.

The book has been written after conducting detailed research and ethnographic interviews with shapers, young global leaders and other forum constituents. Utkarsh explores themes such as emotional intelligence, adaptability quotient and mental health in the context of the modern workplace. He has added concrete examples from his experience of being a Global Shaper, founding Network Capital and working with technology companies and non-profits.

An important point of focus for the book is radical collaboration. Every day, I witness different stakeholders collaborating across age groups, regions, religions and boundaries, and it makes it clear to me that such a collaborative approach is essential for addressing complex challenges of the 21st century. We must move from a world that prioritizes materialism to a human-centred world with inter-generational perspectives. Utkarsh's focus on peer-to-peer learning and sharing is a good example of how we can build robust collaboration principles at work that can be scaled to other domains as well.

2020 was the 50th anniversary of World Economic Forum's Annual Meeting in Davos. While there were many debates and discussions around the challenging state of global affairs, our focus was to establish stakeholder capitalism as a way of addressing the world's greatest challenges, from societal divisions created by income inequality and political polarization to the climate crisis we face today. It was energizing to learn that businesses are now fully embracing the stakeholder capitalism, which means not only maximizing profits but using their capabilities and resources in cooperation with governments and civil societies to address the key issues of this decade. They must actively contribute to a more cohesive and sustainable world.

Utkarsh's work explains why the world demands a new kind of 'advanced' business leader who makes conscious attempts to find meaningful work, create opportunities for others and solve problems beyond the bottom line. That's the spirit of being a Global Shaper and I am glad Utkarsh has put forward crisp mental models and operating principles for people committed to leading from the front.

Klaus Schwab,
Founder and Executive Chairman,
World Economic Forum

Preface

Ikigai (生き甲斐, pronounced [ikigai]) is a Japanese concept that means 'a reason for being'. It is seen as the convergence of four primary elements:

- What you love
- What you are good at
- What the world needs
- What you can get paid for

As a mechanical engineer who spent a significant portion of his undergraduate education pursuing theatre and parliamentary debating, I often struggled to figure out how to balance my passions with conventional career wisdom. Gradually I realized the importance of creating a tribe of mentors and made conscious efforts to add value to their lives and proactively learn from them. This growing tribe of mentors helped me navigate some of the most intricate professional and personal challenges. Case in point—when I broke my left arm on a bitterly cold night in New York bang in the middle of the placement season in business school. They inspired me by their generosity and commitment to my growth. They helped me formulate some of the most important questions. They challenged me, comforted me and unconsciously planted the seeds of 'Ikigai' in my life.

I believe that the secret to a fulfilling life and a meaningful career is the relentless pursuit of Ikigai. Unfortunately, most schools and colleges around the world are designed to crush it. 21st century educational institutions still operate on the 18th century factory-based model of standardizing aspirations, creativity, pursuits and dreams. The most glaring side effect is that students and young professionals make career choices based on insufficient information and insights. They spend way too little time figuring out their strengths, weaknesses, dreams and aspirations, and way too much time trying to crack the code of professional success—exams, appraisals and trends.

I am trying to alter the alchemy of career exploration through my peer mentoring community Network Capital. Our adventure of being a 100,000+ strong mentoring force across 104 countries is fuelled by 'trust leaps'. We exchange ideas, insights and feedback with fellow community members we know nothing about apart from the fact they are partners in crime in our mission to democratize inspiration and make best-in-class mentoring accessible to every person. In a world obsessed with building walls and firewalls, we are committed to building bridges that transcend differences of nationality, culture, conviction, political belief and orientation.

Fundamentally, building communities is about nurturing values and developing shared ownership among members. In creating effective mentor–mentee pairs, we use a chatbot and other aspects of conversational Artificial Intelligence but our true strength is the breadth, depth, versatility and diversity of our community.

Network Capital started as a social experiment to explore whether young professionals having vastly different political beliefs, diplomatic orientations and convictions can serve as peer mentors. It turns out they can—in the first three months we saw mentor–mentee pairs across India–Pakistan, Iran–Israel, Russia–Ukraine, to name a few. They were not 'tolerating' each other. They were relishing learning with and from each other.

The success of our experiment gave us confidence to scale and build a truly inclusive skill sharing and peer mentoring community open to all who have the hunger to learn and willingness to share. I believe that every single person has something to learn and something to share. From day one, we focused on building a culture of radical collaboration and forging meaningful partnerships to inspire innovation and enable skill-sharing at scale.

To share an example, Network Capital partnered with NITI Aayog (Government of India's premier policy think tank) for *Atal Innovation Mission*, as part of which highly skilled and motivated young professionals mentor students in the Atal Tinkering Labs set up under the Mission, across the country. Through such partnerships, we aspire to democratize inspiration and bridge the gap between boardrooms and classrooms.

Eighty-five per cent of the jobs in the year 2030 haven't been imagined yet, and we are just getting started with the fourth Industrial Revolution. I believe that in future most people will be 'career entrepreneurs'. They will monetize their unique skills on the global market instead of seeking conventional employment. We are already seeing that happen. This book will present many such examples.

The pursuit of careers will undergo tectonic changes and students, professionals, employers and educational institutions will need to adapt. They will have to learn and unlearn consistently and efficiently. This is, of course, easier said than done. Change, especially when it comes from all directions at breakneck speed, is unsettling. That is why we need to comfort people and give them confidence.

What started off as a social experiment has matured into a global community providing personalized career guidance to over 100,000 people. We got here without spending a single dollar on marketing. My role as the Founder and Chief Culture Officer of Network Capital is to ensure that we remain true to our founding principle, remember who we are and what we stand for.

Master community builder and serial entrepreneur, Caterina Fake, quoted during a show called *Masters of Scale*, 'What you tolerate is who you are.' Walking past a downtown Seattle coffee shop, I saw a huge canvas that summarized what we will never tolerate, the precise quote was: 'No Sexism, Racism, Ableism, Homophobia, Transphobia or General Hatefulness. You will be asked to leave.'

Network Capital aspires to help build meaningful careers and inspire 'Ikigai' in everyone, but one Network Capital is not enough. We need many. We are blessed to have brilliant community members who are leading similar initiatives for refugees, people with physical disabilities, veterans, among others. Giving wings to the dreams and aspirations of these micro-communities is of paramount importance to us. We are taking baby steps—inch by inch, play by play.

HOW TO USE THIS BOOK

It takes way more than hard work to succeed. In fact, misdirected hard work is way worse than no work at all. Our society has constantly exaggerated the role of hard work and underplayed the critical role of choices and mentorship in creating conditions for success. That is why we have such a large chunk of students and young professionals who work very hard but accomplish very little.

This book is divided into six parts: Principles of Shaping a Meaningful Career; Building a Tribe of Mentors; Navigating the Modern Workplace: Millennial Matters; Augmenting Personal Productivity; Learning from the Best; and Clarity is Power: Mental Models and the Art of Deep Thinking. Each part has several sub-units that end with practical takeaways and tips for everyday life.

While the takeaways are self-explanatory, you should consider going through the examples and research presented in the units. I have drawn upon and extensively quoted from my weekly columns in *Mint*, examples from Network Capital and insights from some of the best professors, entrepreneurs, writers, activists and artists which will hopefully make your learning adventure worth it.

As you uncover different concepts presented in the book, feel free to complement and contextualize them with examples from your own life. You don't need to agree with all the findings and suggestions. Use the insights here as guiding principles for personal reflection.

Your personal takeaway from every section will be different from mine. That is why I have added a box titled 'Key Takeaways' after every chapter. You should use this section for taking notes and jotting down relevant examples from your life. I don't have all the answers and I am not the ultimate source of millennial wisdom. All I hope for is that you relate to some of my adventures and experiments. The ultimate measure of success will be if my curiosity resonates with yours. Let's get started.

Acknowledgements

I always enjoyed writing, but I think I became a writer in Italy.

One night, lost in the 'profound' depths of my social media feed, I missed a stop from Venice to Florence and found myself in Bologna. With all hotel rooms booked out and the next train scheduled for morning, I decided to walk around and direct my own version of *Midnight in Paris* in Bologna.

After that night, writing became an integral part of my life. I started following my curiosity and my pen became my mentor. I was able to capture my adventures and misadventures with some objectivity and some wonder; thanks largely to the extended support system I was able to build over the years.

It is impossible to name everyone, so I am going to stick to experiences that shaped me. The people who made it happen know who they are, and this book is largely a result of their love.

Although I built a community for learning and networking, some of the most meaningful relationships have been a result of serendipity. As I discuss in the book, my 'luck surface area' and that of thousands of other Network Capital members grew because we were exposed to meaningful new opportunities every day. For me, one such opportunity was the weekly column at *Mint*.

This book would not have happened without my *Mint* column and the *Mint* column would not have happened without the Network Capital community member who connected me to the editor there after reading one of my World Economic Forum articles titled 'How to Find a Job You Love'. My article gave her the clarity to leave the dreary job she was in. She thanked me with a precious introduction, and I am grateful for that. Today she is doing terrific as an entrepreneur.

I have been blessed to be part of several iconic institutions and communities. This book captures some of my experiences and those of my peers and mentors. Without their insights and generosity of spirit, I would not have been able to capture the complexity of work life.

As my life became busier than usual in the last few years, writing emerged as my tool for reflection and synthesis. It helped me cut through the clutter and stumble into clarity. This was far from being a solitary pursuit. My grandparents read everything I wrote and provided feedback that helped make the book relevant to people of all age groups. They shared detailed comments with vintage ink pens and eventually embraced digital mediums. Now they get to know where I am published before anyone else and share it fondly on their social media feeds.

I come from a family where the pursuit of knowledge is the most important life goal. Home has always been thousands of books spread around, waiting to be explored with a fresh set of eyes. Growing up in such an environment helped; I didn't need to wander around for inspiration. I picked up a strong work ethic from my parents and little brother. To give you an example, I do not remember a day where I woke up and did not find my mother with a book in her hand, writing furiously on its margins.

Over the course of writing this book, I got a chance to travel to 40 countries and innumerable cities: from the CEO roundtables in Davos to the business school summits in Boston, Detroit and Cairo, to the unmatched wonders of Casablanca, Oxford and Fontainebleau. Travel helped me build Network Capital communities around the world and discover who I am. Many stories captured in this book are a direct consequence of the exposure I got from my travels.

What are stories without people and what are people without communities? Big shout out to the people and communities who have translated this book from being a medley of happenstances to a compendium of stories sprinkled with practical insights and mental models. I deserve no credit for these stories. If I did something well, it was to find these gems of people, especially one French–Lebanese computer scientist whom I met after a long, meandering afternoon on The Great Wall of China. She said, 'You should write.' I followed her advice.

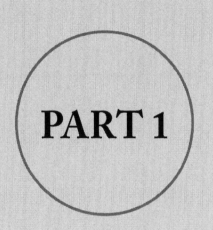

PART 1

PRINCIPLES OF SHAPING A MEANINGFUL CAREER

CHAPTER 1

DON'T FOLLOW YOUR PASSION

Like many millennials, I have often received career advice along the lines of 'follow your passion', which roughly translates to following my inner, inexplicable, hard to control calling. Although it sounds great, it is hard to understand, deconstruct and put into practise. Recently, Stanford's Carol Dweck, asked her students, 'How many of you are waiting to find your passion?'

One can't help but notice the dissonance between the emphasis on passion at work and the lack of avenues to build meaningful careers. What Dweck asked her students is a common refrain in society. The usage of the phrase 'follow your passion' has increased nine-fold in English books since the 1990s.

As a student or a young professional, it can be deeply unsettling to be bombarded with 'follow your passion' kind of advice. How are we supposed to follow our passion without any institutional, cultural or systemic encouragement, career support or mentoring?

Usually we don't discover our passion by sitting under a tree and waiting for the metaphoric apple to fall.

Dweck and Greg Walton published a paper in *Psychological Science* where they argue that passions aren't found, they are nurtured and developed over time with the help of micro-experiments, grit and resilience. If we quit every time we find a stumbling block and blame it on lack of passion, we are in for a rough ride.

For me, micro-experiments have helped discover my strengths, likes and dislikes. They have helped me come up with an informed and experiential discovery of myself. I have realized three things.

First, passions, likes and dislikes can change over a period of time. Second, we constantly underestimate the change we will go through. Third, accepting change gets harder every year.

One of the most important skills in the 21st century will be the ability to continually reinvent oneself. Even with the best of technologies, available free of cost, it is very hard and profoundly lonely to do this alone. That's why we need to build and be part of diverse learning communities. Network Capital is one such example among hundreds of others.

When I started Network Capital, I cared about building communities, but that wasn't the only thing I was passionate about. Through the thousands of hours of experimentation and work, I found my calling. The big takeaway for me was that hard work, tinkering and experimentation preceded the discovery of passion.

I have deep respect for people who figured out what they wanted to do early in life, but for the rest of us, let's abandon the wild goose chase of passion. Instead, let's follow our curiosity and tinker away to success—with our community who will be cheering us through our adventures.

Key Takeaways

- Passions are developed, not found.
- Passions evolve over time.
- Focusing on curiosity and purpose is far more rewarding than waiting for your passion.
- You won't be able to find your passion alone.
- Form and be part of learning communities.

CHAPTER 2

WHY 'BE YOURSELF' IS BAD CAREER ADVICE

Be Yourself is a well-meaning, yet confusing, advice millennials get all the time. Perhaps because we live in the age where even intelligence is artificial, the quest for authenticity has never been higher. We want to work for authentic companies, pursue projects with authentic colleagues, report to authentic managers and be with authentic friends.

Pretending to be someone you are not can be excruciatingly exhausting. More so, people can tell when someone is putting on a show. It is impossible to wear a mask for 12 hours a day, five days a week. Even if you manage, it is unlikely that your colleagues will trust you. Without trust, there is no cooperation and without cooperation, the entire premise of the modern, collaborative work environment falls apart.

Two Arizona based professors, Jennifer Parth and Richard Kinnier, used content analysis from 90 American University commencement speeches delivered between 1990 and 2007. Unsurprisingly, one of the most frequently used messages was *Be Yourself*. A whopping 48 per cent of speakers referenced it in some form.

Knowing yourself is hard work, especially when you are young. That's the time when no one listens to you, everyone has stray bits of advice and you feel the pressure to meet unreasonable expectations.

Further, *Be Yourself* assumes that there is one fixed self that you have to discover and unleash upon the rest of the world. This is categorically false because we have the tendency to underestimate the personal and contextual change we go through. In fact, Stanford Psychology Professor Carol Dweck's research on mindset has shown that believing that there is a fixed self can interfere with personal and professional growth.

That is why, instead of trying to be your fixed self all the time, you should consider micro-experiments that can help you know yourself and your leadership style. It obviously doesn't mean that you show up to work as a different person each week. All I am saying is that as long as you stick to your core values, it is worth tinkering with different strokes of authentic leadership.

In today's interconnected, global work environments, we have to negotiate with all kinds of people on a daily basis. It is unreasonable to expect everyone to adapt to our style just because we feel the need to express without restraint. Authenticity does not mean insensitivity and doesn't give us the license to be brash.

Believing in the tyranny of the fixed, authentic, unrestrained self can also land you in serious trouble. *Esquire's* editor A.J. Jacobs tinkered with radical honesty and spent a few weeks trying to be fully authentic. In this period, he frightened a five-year-old girl when she commented on his yellow teeth, told his mother-in-law that the birthday gift she sent was ridiculous, announced to a nanny that he would go on a date with her if he were single and confessed to his wife that he often confused her with his sister. You can imagine how this experiment worked out for Jacobs. This is what he said after the culmination of the experiment—'Deceit makes our world go round. Without lies, marriages would crumble, workers would be fired, egos would be shattered, governments would collapse.'

I completely disagree with Jacobs' simplistic quote but I think his experiment helps us uncover nuances of authenticity and efficacy. Adapting content to context is not equal to being less authentic or disingenuous. It simply shows you have the humility to experiment.

Wharton's organizational psychologist, Adam Grant, explains that instead of searching for our inner selves and then figuring out a way to express them, one should start with our outer selves. He suggests that we should pay attention to how we present ourselves to others, and then try to be the people we claim to be.

Instead of obsessing over authenticity, one should recognize that knowing oneself is a tough task and focus on building a growth mindset that is hungry to learn and unlearn.

Key Takeaways

- We don't have one fixed self.
- Micro-experiments will help you understand your various selves.
- Experimenting to figure out who you are doesn't make you less authentic.
- Pay close attention to how you present yourself to others, observe personal hypocrisies and work backwards.
- What you do is who you are.

CHAPTER 3

BUBBLES OF COMPETENCE

Sir Arthur Conan Doyle created Sherlock Holmes. Surprisingly, he was fooled by two school girls who claimed to have photographed fairies frolicking around the park. Albert Einstein came up with the equation of mass–energy equivalence. He also wasted the last 25 years of his career with a string of embarrassing failures. His Princeton colleagues started avoiding him as he knowingly ignored experiment results and well-known facts. Thomas Edison had more than 1,000 patents to his name but he waged a misguided war on alternating current even though he knew he was wrong. How is it that such smart people made such unfortunate choices?

In his book, *The Intelligence Trap*, David Robinson explains that no one is universally smart. We all operate in our own bubbles of competence. Being smart or gifted doesn't make us immune to bias. In fact, it can magnify them. Arthur Conan Doyle started dabbling in his extra-terrestrial adventures at the same time he created Sherlock Holmes. He used his intelligence to come up with creative arguments to dismiss his sceptics and justify his whacky beliefs.

Let's explore the contours of motivated reasoning, the technique Conan Doyle used to outsmart himself. It is an emotionally charged, self-protective use of our minds that takes two distinct forms. First, we preferentially seek and remember information that confirms to our world view. Second, we tear down reasonable, alternate arguments and become entrenched in our own cherished opinions. Smart people like Edison, Doyle and Einstein are particularly prone to this aspect of motivated reasoning called disconfirmation bias.

That's why I think there is a fundamental flaw in how we measure intelligence. Colleagues we refer to as smart tend to have high scores in standardized tests, demonstrate good abstract thinking and are known for effortless logical reasoning. We admire them and start relying on their judgement without question. This is where trouble begins.

Intelligence, in its narrow sense, has a modest correlation with rationality. A study published by London School of Economics found that people with higher intelligence quotient (IQ) tend to consume more alcohol or are, maybe, more likely to smoke or take illegal drugs. Obviously, it doesn't mean that if you drink and smoke a lot, you have a high IQ, but it does imply that smart people often make unwise decisions.

Karen Ho's *Ethnography of Wall Street* analysed behavioural patterns and decision-making frameworks of investment bankers during the 2008 financial crisis. The conclusion drawn from the analysis implied that, if anything, the higher collective IQ of Wall Street left the world worse off.

Bertrand Russel famously said that the cause of trouble is that in the modern world, the stupid are cocksure while the intelligent are full of doubt. I feel such pronouncements can be thoroughly confusing. They incorrectly assume that people are born stupid or smart.

Cognitive psychology's Dunning–Kruger effect states that confidence and competence have a complicated relationship. It was inspired by the case of McArthur Wheeler who tried to rob two banks in broad daylight. He was genuinely perplexed on being caught. It turns out that he believed that a coating of lemon juice would make him invisible in the CCTV footage. Unsurprisingly, the Dunning–Kruger effect is often used to explain why incompetent people have delusions of grandeur.

However, there is a silver lining. It turns out that education and training improve not only our knowledge but also our metacognition and self-awareness. It doesn't mean that reading a few books on relativity will make you an Einstein, but it does suggest that with increased self-awareness, you have it in you to stumble upon your bubble of competence. With perseverance and the right kind of exploratory support, you can transform perceived incompetence into competence you truly care about.

Intelligence is a discovery challenge. Your colleague who is lost during sales calls could be a genius in programming. Instead of mentally branding him as stupid, help him discover his bubble of competence. On a different day, in a different context, he will do the same for you.

Key Takeaways
- No one is universally smart. We all operate in bubbles of competence.
- Intelligence has modest correlation with rationality.
- Confidence and competence have a complicated relationship.
- Education and training improve knowledge and self-awareness.
- Intelligence is a discovery challenge.

CHAPTER 4

ART OF BEING A DEEP GENERALIST

Tennis star Roger Federer dabbled with basketball, handball, skiing, wrestling, swimming, table tennis and skateboarding as a kid. When he began to gravitate towards tennis, his parents cautioned him against taking the sport too seriously. Essentially, when they discovered his love for sports, they encouraged him to have what author Dave Epstein calls a sampling period—low risk experiments meant to organically discover what one loves doing and most wants to succeed in.

Golf legend Tiger Woods, on the other hand, specialized under his father's tutelage before he turned three. Wood's learning path of early specialization has become the default template for schools and colleges that want to prime students for excellence. Even in most modern workplaces, a disproportionate emphasis is paid on having narrow skills that are marketable. While there is nothing wrong in having an area of focus, one should be mindful of the perils of early specialization. There are three key reasons for that.

First, we tend to specialize without knowing why. More than 80 per cent of people work in areas that have nothing to do with their field of study. In India, for example, most students first graduate from courses like engineering and then figure out what they want to do with their lives. Spending four years of one's life getting deep into a subject one doesn't particularly care about is a colossal waste of time, energy and money.

Second, it hinders lateral thinking, a problem-solving approach that draws upon seemingly disparate concepts and domains. Most innovators are lateral thinkers. Their lateral thinking is a direct result of combining different strands of thoughts and learning from different contexts. Leonardo Da Vinci combined art and engineering, Steve Jobs built upon the interconnectedness of design, fashion and technology and Richard Feynman, a Nobel Laureate in Physics, is known to draw upon references from music.

Third, people with a narrow set of skills tend to approach every problem through the same lens. This not only ignores loopholes in one's hypothesis but also amplifies biases. As investor—Charlie Munger—often quotes 'To a man with a hammer, everything looks like a nail.'

So, if early specialization can backfire, should we all snack on an array of ideas, insights and interests? The short answer is no. The future belongs to deep generalists, a term popularized by JotForm's CEO, Aytekin Tank. These are people who combine two or more diverse domains and integrate them into something defensible and unique.

In the 21st century, with the mainstreaming of automation and artificial intelligence (AI), some jobs will be automated and some would become redundant. Even highly trained and accomplished professionals—radiologists, traders, programmers, etc.—might lose their jobs to algorithms if they are over-reliant on their narrow set of specialized skills.

On the other hand, deep generalists not only will keep their jobs but will also be able to demand a premium for what they bring to the table. These are the professionals who will push the boundaries of creativity and innovation in the AI era. Their competitive advantage—a unique combination of breadth and depth—will propel them to learn, unlearn and develop innovative solutions consistently.

One of the best professional decisions I took in my early twenties was to invest a year studying liberal arts at Ashoka University. I was part of the first cohort of Young India Fellowship where 57 of us learned the art of connecting ideas from different walks of life. Studying anthropology, philosophy, history, literature, art and economics after a couple of years of work experience helped me understand what I wanted to do and why. Most importantly, it set me on the path to becoming a deep generalist by strengthening my lateral thinking ability. This is of course clearer in retrospect. I didn't pursue the fellowship to become a generalist or a specialist. I was simply following my curiosity.

I chose to take a year out to study before heading for my MBA at INSEAD Business School but there are many other ways to achieve the same goal. As long as we can figure out a way to build or be a part of diverse learning communities, we can conduct several low-risk professional experiments to sample various options and double-down on ones that interest us. I am not saying that sampling will make all of us like Roger Federer or Richard Feynman but it will position us to make thoughtful career decisions.

In the age of widespread automation, learning and unlearning will be a lifelong pursuit. Tools and technologies will constantly change. While this might unsettle those with a narrow set of skills, it will empower deep generalists to create new opportunities they have nurtured over years for building lateral thinking and conducting repeated experiments to figure how they want to contribute to the ever-changing world around them.

Key Takeaways

- Sampling period is essential to discover areas that pique our interest. Once we conduct several rounds of low-risk experiments, we figure out what we are good at and what problems we wish to solve.
- Specializing without knowing why or simply because someone said so could seriously backfire.
- The future belongs to deep generalists, those who combine two or more diverse domains and integrate them into something defensible and unique.
- Following one's curiosity is one of the most effective ways to become a deep generalist.
- We can't become deep generalists on our own. In addition to following our curiosity, we need to create or be part of diverse learning communities.

CHAPTER 5

HOW CONFUSION LEADS TO PERSONAL AND PROFESSIONAL GROWTH

I have met many people who are confused about what they want to do with their lives but I am yet to meet someone who feels happy about it. Essentially, confusion is grappling with uncertain, ambiguous situations where there is a dissonance between expectation and reality. Confusion occurs because our prior experiences—academic, professional and social—leave us unprepared to deal with new situations that are bound to come up every so often.

While confusion can be crippling in the short term, it is a vital tool for personal growth. It can help discover what we really want to do and make sense of the world around.

An associate professor at University of Notre Dame, Dr Sidney D'Mello, suggests that confusion augments learning if it is properly induced, effectively regulated and ultimately resolved. He found that students who dealt with uncertainty triggered by contradictions scored higher on a difficult post-test and could more successfully identify flaws in new case studies. Given the research findings, should we intentionally confuse ourselves in order to strengthen our thought process and mental models?

It turns out that there is a three-pronged framework to leverage confusion and make it work for us.

First, be productively confused instead of hopelessly confused. In a classroom, productive confusion occurs when the source of the confusion is closely linked to the content of the learning session. This happens when the learning ecosystem provides concrete help when students are struggling. At work, it means that our confusions can be resolved with the help of peers and overall office support system.

Without guided mentorship, confusion can become debilitating and make things worse. In such situations, we need to analyse if we have the necessary tools to eventually figure things out. If even after repeated attempts, we are unable to navigate a problem-solving approach that has some probability of success, it is time to ask for help or change our operating context. Yes, in certain cases that means looking for a new job within or outside your organization.

Second, manage negative emotions when they occur. Dealing with ambiguity can take a toll on our well-being if we start taking things personally. This is of course easier said than done. It is worth keeping in mind that the occasional bad day is a natural by-product of dealing with complexity. We need to separate the problem at hand and our warped perspective due to the emotional roller coaster we have just gone through. We can't let it get to us.

Third, be willing to risk failure. While dealing with unfamiliar situations is likely to make us resilient and strengthen our decision-making faculties, it isn't a guaranteed outcome. We need to be open to embracing the occasional failure. It is a fair price to pay for the accelerated learning it offers.

For the longest time I used to resent myself for being confused about my personal and professional life. I would compare my life to the glittering lives of peers on social media and wonder how they were all so sorted. It was only after years of introspection that I realized that envy and confusion were great equalizers: We all experience and deal with them in different shapes and forms.

My life changed for the better the day I accepted that my confusion was perhaps a step towards learning and self-discovery. I took heart from the fact that great scientists and philosophers dedicated their lives to negotiating with the spectre of confusion. A professor of Biomedical Engineering at Yale University, Martin Schwartz, once wrote that if we don't feel stupid and confused, it means we are not really trying.

As someone who has never been shy of trying, I realized that without confusion, it was impossible to stumble into truth. In a way, being chronically confused made the pursuit to clarity worth it to me.

To a certain degree, I am still confused and perhaps will always be, but the difference between my former and current self is that I don't feel I have to deal with it alone. I have helped build and been part of several communities where young professionals have garnered enough trust that they can be open about their successes and failures. Over time, we managed to embrace confusion as a collective.

Knowing that others were in the same boat and attempting to help fellow community members figure out a path to clarity turned out to be an immensely fulfilling experience. In a way, it shaped my career and turned out to be a super-power.

Key Takeaways
- Confusion can be crippling in the short term but is essential for personal growth.
- Strive to be productively confused.
- Manage negative emotions as and when they occur.
- Don't feel compelled to deal with your confusion alone.
- Share your confusion and push others to think through their confusions.

CHAPTER 6

WHY EARLY FAILURES IN OUR CAREER SET US UP FOR LONG-TERM SUCCESS

American Supreme Court's Chief Justice, John Roberts, delivered an unusual commencement address at his son's ninth-grade graduation. Among other things, he wished the students bad luck and hoped that they fail enough to learn from their misfortunes. It turns out that bad luck and early failures set us up for success.

Benjamin Jones and Dashun Yang from Kellogg School of Management researched the impact of early career setbacks on future career impact and found three counter-intuitive trends. First, early professional setback has a strong and permanent negative impact on a small set of people. In Jones and Yang's sample set, about 10 per cent of the people permanently disappeared after initial failure. They never tried again.

Second, those who experience an early setback tend to outperform their peers if they keep trying. Jones and Yang compared those who narrowly missed achieving their goal with those who just crossed the threshold for success. Over a period of time, the individuals who managed failure with consistent effort did far better than those who achieved early success.

Third, early-career setback improves performance among those who persevere. Jones and Yang call it the 'what doesn't kill you makes you stronger' effect.

Entrepreneurs and venture capitalists (VCs) have a lot to learn from their research. Almost 75 per cent of venture capital backed start-ups fail to return money to investors. In the Indian context, according to a research conducted by the International Business Machines Corporation (IBM) and Oxford, 9 out of every 10 start-ups fail in the first five years of operation. VCs love founders with strong track records. That is why every time a founder with a successful exit decides to start a company, they are brimming with offers of funding from investors. While there is nothing wrong with this, VCs are missing out on a huge pool of talent.

Instead of running after a handful number of hyper-successful entrepreneurs, they should keep an eye on founders they thought of investing in but didn't. The VC world is small. One can quickly get a list of companies that have been rejected by their peers. This consolidated list can be a useful guide for future investments.

Drawing upon Jones and Yang's research, we will see a small percentage of entrepreneurs who will never try after a few rejections. However, there would be some who, despite all rejections, kept trying, solicited feedback, improved customer experience and built something meaningful. These are the hidden gems investors should reconsider because they didn't let initial set of failures daunt them. In fact, they got better with each rejection.

If you are an entrepreneur, you will fail multiple times and failure will feel far more personal as compared to an investor. At times you may feel like the unluckiest person alive and be tempted to give up. That's when you should take your luck in your own hands.

Serial entrepreneur Jason Roberts inadvertently coined the phrase 'Luck Surface Area' during a discussion on his podcast *TechZing*. Roberts explains that we can hack serendipity and make ourselves lucky. Instead of being subject to the whims and fancies of luck, we can create our destiny.

He formalized the concept into the equation L = D × T, where '*L*' is luck, '*D*' is doing and '*T*' is telling.

Luck Surface Area is directly proportional to excellence and influence. We need to get better at our craft and tell lots of people about it.

It is important to keep in mind that passion is not enough for excellence. However, we tend to work harder for things we truly care about. Because our work is channelled, the output per hour is greater and we get much better at our craft.

As we get better, more people get to know about our pursuits and tell their friends. Network effects set it. Our friends knowing about our work isn't enough. We need to reach out to different networks, communities and organizations. New opportunities often come from surprising places. We call such happenstances serendipity, but actually they are merely the expansion of our luck surface area.

When we fail or experience hard luck, we should draw inspiration from Jones and Yang's research or Chief Justice John Roberts' convocation speech. The setback or stroke of misfortune might be positioning us for long-term success. All we need to do is not give up after a string of initial failures and keep expanding our luck surface area.

Key Takeaways

- Early professional setback has a strong and permanent negative impact on a small set of people.
- Those who experience an early setback tend to outperform their peers if they keep trying.
- Early-career setback improves performance among those who persevere.
- If you want to back talent, look where no one is looking: those who narrowly missed their goals but kept trying.
- You can hack luck. $L = D \times T$, where 'L' is luck, 'D' is doing and 'T' is telling.

CHAPTER 7

WHY AQ MATTERS MORE THAN IQ AND EQ

Yangyang Cheng is an auditor turned stand-up comic who moved to the United States to teach Chinese at Pepperdine University. Soon after, she became a household name in China as the host of the hit TV show *Hollywood Lifestyle*. Today, she is the co-founder of YoYo Chinese, an educational technology (edutech) company that has helped almost a million English speakers learn Mandarin online. There is no doubt that Cheng is smart but her competitive advantage is her adaptability quotient or AQ, the ability to change course and repivot in response to unanticipated changes.

For years, it was thought that the Intelligence Quotient (IQ) test—which measures analytical and mathematical ability—was the most accurate way to predict performance on the job. Then in the late 1990s, we witnessed the emotional intelligence boom, with scholars like Daniel Goleman explaining how we'd been over-indexing on analytical abilities and ignoring relational aspects of work.

While both IQ and EQ are still important in the 21st century, it is our AQ that will determine how well we do at work. The good news is that AQ isn't fixed. There is a way to learn from the future as it emerges.

The founder of MIT's Presencing Institute, Otto Scharmer, has developed a framework for strengthening adaptability of both, individuals and organizations. His research suggests that we can strengthen our AQ by focusing on three core elements: open mind, open heart and open will.

First, keeping an open mind propels us to see the world with a fresh set of eyes and remain open to new possibilities. Following this approach also ensures that our bias doesn't colour our learning experience.

While learning from past mistakes and experiences is important, it doesn't necessarily prepare us for future challenges in a world where the operating context is continually changing. That is why nudging ourselves to embrace the unknown without judgement is critical to building AQ.

Second, embracing new adventures with an open heart augments our empathy and empowers us with fresh perspective. Radical collaboration would be an essential skill for most jobs in the 21st century. We will have to learn to work with teams that constantly change in terms of structure, culture and composition. The ability to see any situation through another person's eyes will help us forge meaningful networks essential for career advancement.

The third component of building our AQ is keeping an open will. This entails letting go of ego and embracing discomfort of the unknown. This is of course easier said than done. As we get more experience and develop expertise, starting afresh is challenging. Our identity and personal brand are built over years of consistent work, and maintaining status quo is tempting. In moments like these we must remember that failing to evolve can spell doom for professional growth. The same things that made us successful in the past can be totally irrelevant in a different context.

Evolving doesn't mean abandoning everything that worked for us. Microsoft's CEO, Satya Nadella's book, *Hit Refresh,* offers a useful mental model. He suggests that we should strive to retain elements of our past that gave us meaning and let go of baggage that weighs us down.

In the year 2000, Netflix's co-founder Reed Hastings met with John Antioco, the CEO of Blockbuster. He proposed a partnership to manage Blockbuster's fledgling online business. At the time Blockbuster was the undisputed market leader with millions of existing customers and thousands of money-minting retail stores. John barely heard Reed. He was promptly laughed out of the room.

Ten years after that meeting, Blockbuster filed for bankruptcy and Netflix's valuation jumped to over USD 10 billion. Goldman Sachs' Natalie Fratto explains that there is constant tension between exploration and exploitation. Like John Antioco, most of us tend to overvalue exploitation at the cost of developing our future selves. Now let's contrast John with Yangyang Cheng who kept hitting refresh. Without getting too attached to her success, she made adaptability a core component of her identity. This enabled her to carve out a meaningful career, riddled with adventures and insured for future.

Consciously working towards building AQ will give you the motivation to learn, unlearn and relearn. AQ alone may not make you successful but a lack of it will ensure failure in the modern workplace.

Key Takeaways

- IQ and EQ are both important in the 21st century but not nearly as important as AQ, our ability to change course and reinvent oneself.
- AQ isn't fixed. There is a way to learn from the future as it emerges.
- We can strengthen our AQ by focusing on keeping an open mind, open heart and open will.
- 'Hit Refresh' often: Retain meaningful elements of the past and let go of unnecessary baggage.

CHAPTER 8

WHAT GRANDMOTHERS TEACH US ABOUT REINVENTING ONESELF

Vicky Bennison read Zoology in college and graduated with an MBA from University of Bath. Thereafter, she worked in international development across Siberia, South Africa and Turkmenistan. Today, she is best known as the person behind *Pasta Grannies*, a YouTube channel that finds and films real Italian grannies—nonne—making traditional, handmade pasta.

These grannies make lip-smacking pasta and tell delightful stories. What amazes me even more is how these grannies have embraced social media, learned digital marketing and emerged as media entrepreneurs—all around the world.

Closer home, we have the example of Mastanamma, the world's oldest celebrity chef who got her big break at the age of 105 years when her grandson filmed her cooking eggplant curry and put it online. She had cataract, wore dentures, cooked outside on an open fire and sometimes roasted chicken inside a steaming watermelon. As the New York Times put it, this was all part of the charm. Mastanamma was natural on camera and got over one million subscribers in two years, thereby emerging as a legitimate internet sensation.

These grannies offer precious insights about the future of work, especially the importance of reinventing oneself. Unfortunately, most journals and media reports overemphasize the importance of certain skills without explaining how challenging it gets to acquire them with each passing year. Reinventing our mental models will probably be the most crucial aspect of finding work in the coming years. Let's understand why.

Authors of *100 Year Life*, Lynda Gratton and Andrew Scott, offer three defining features of work in the 21st century. First, people are likely to live much longer. Second, lifespan of organizations will significantly reduce. Third, concept of retirement will fade away, partly due to financial reasons and partly out of choice. Combining all these factors, it is easy to visualize how one might have to learn to work in different industries, sectors and functions every few years.

One of the first things we will see is the disruption of the traditional study, work and retire model by the continual loops of work followed by study. People will probably go to college multiple times in their lives or enrol in a specialized degree at the age of 75 years. It is also possible that college degrees get split into smaller chunks or the whole notion of going to college gets replaced by alternate learning and apprenticeship models. Several venture capital backed companies in Silicon Valley are already tinkering with this idea. While it is difficult to predict whether colleges will survive or alternate learning models will prevail, it is abundantly clear that lifelong learning will be central to all our lives.

Lifelong learning doesn't mean chasing buzzwords, hashtags and latest media obsessions. If we do that, we will be on a perennial wild goose chase because there are way too many new things to catch up on. If we want to become effective lifelong learners, we must figure out ways to connect the dots between what we already know and what we aspire to know. What we aspire to know must follow our curiosity and factor our strengths, interests and time availability.

The Italian grannies and centenarians like Mastanamma were able to succeed because they leveraged their strengths and chose to work on things they truly cared about. They used technology to augment their potential and thoroughly enjoyed the experience of reinventing themselves as cutting edge digital content producers. In addition to income, starting up at the age of 100 years gave them something to look forward to and added more meaning to their lives. If you want to see how this manifests, you can look at Gina Petitti's YouTube video thanking her fans on reaching the 100,000 subscribers milestone.

Videos are of course great but if you prefer a real-life demo, you can meet my grandmother at the India International Centre Library writing chapters of her new book on her tablet. Perhaps Vicky Bennison will consider doing a video series on Indian grannies as well.

Key Takeaways

- Reinventing ourselves is going to be the most important skill of the 21st century.
- The traditional study–work–retire model will make way for lifelong learning.
- Lifelong learning doesn't mean chasing hot buzzwords. It comes down to figuring out the sweet spot between our curiosity and strengths.
- Technology will expand the scope of jobs and create different kinds of economic opportunities.
- Those who invest time in augmenting their skillsets will reap the economic and technological benefits.

CHAPTER 9

TRANSFORMING YOUR ADVERSITY INTO COMPETITIVE EDGE

I met Miguel Centeno at a technology conference in Cairo, few weeks before the global lockdown due to COVID-19. A Cuban refugee who grew up in low-income housing projects, Centeno turned his life around to become a distinguished Sociology Professor at Princeton University. Being stuck in Cairo traffic for hours gave us time to connect and I learned how he overcame abject poverty, lack of relatable mentors and constant negative perception due to his Latin American accent into a competitive advantage.

Centeno exemplifies what organizational psychologists call transformative resilience. Sometimes 'bouncing back' after setbacks doesn't get us anywhere. We need to figure out ways to use our setbacks as opportunities to better operate in, and positively affect, the world around us. Everyone is an underdog in some situation or the other, so transforming negative perceptions into positive outcomes is a necessary life skill.

Dr Laura Huang, the author of *Edge: Turning Adversity into Advantage*, suggests that each of us has the power to control how we are perceived by others even when those perceptions are rooted in bias. After studying hundreds of Olympians, corporate executives and entrepreneurs including the likes of Elon Musk,

Dr Huang has put forward a three-pronged approach to flip stereotypes and perceptions.

First, figure out your unique edge and learn to surprise your stakeholders. Working hard isn't enough. We need to learn to add specific value to our stakeholders and add an element of surprise/delight to our endeavours. This begins by knowing ourselves and understanding what we bring to the table.

'Get out of my office,' said Elon Musk when he first saw Dr Huang. He had mistaken the gift in her hand to be a product prototype. Thinking that she was an entrepreneur looking to raise money, Musk asked her to leave his office without giving it a second thought. It was obviously an awkward moment but instead of getting flustered, Dr Huang nervously laughed and cracked a joke. The meeting concluded with bouts of hysterical laughter and Musk offering introductions and connections she couldn't have dreamed of. Dr Huang had managed to gain an edge over one of the most powerful men in the world by surprising him in a moment of massive awkwardness.

Second, deliberately guide assumptions about your worth. Dr Huang has studied the venture capital space and found a wide range of uncomfortable truths. Women receive only two per cent of venture funding, attractive men get funded far more than unattractive men and people with non-standard accents have a particularly hard time getting VCs to back them.

While it is illegal to discriminate based on gender, race or accent, VCs subconsciously justify their funding choices based on intangible aspects like networks, interpersonal influence, political capital etc. These are the things that minorities, women and people with accents tend to be rated lowest on.

When encountering such meetings or situations, one must address the elephant in the room upfront by providing specific examples of overcoming perceived negative biases. This needs to be done tactfully, at the appropriate time and in a benign way.

Third, help people see your future potential. When people make snap judgements, it is never based on a static quality. They project where we are likely to be in future, form a perception and figure how to react. This instant cognitive calculus matters because most people take important decisions based on snap judgements. That is why it is critical that we guide people, especially those unfamiliar with us, about who we are, how we will add value to them and what our growth trajectory will look like.

On the last day of the Cairo conference, Dr Centeno and I discussed meritocracy and privilege in detail. He said that in an ideal world there should be structures in place that guarantee equality of opportunities. Unfortunately, we don't live in an ideal world. While we wait for these structures to change, we should empower ourselves by transforming our adversity into our competitive edge.

Key Takeaways

- Everyone is an underdog is some situation so transforming negative perceptions into positive outcomes is a necessary life skill.
- Figure out your unique edge and learn to surprise your stakeholders.
- Deliberately guide assumptions about your worth.
- Help people see your future potential.
- You can make your adversity your edge by embodying transformative resilience.

CHAPTER 10

AN ODE TO MEDIOCRITY

Do you remember the last time you pursued a hobby or passion solely for pleasure, no strings attached? As we surrender our lives to the altar of hustle, even leisure and relaxation have become competitive sports. Even while pursuing our hobbies we feel compelled to prove a point—to ourselves and our friends—that we are indeed having a great time and winning the race of life.

Columbia University law professor Tim Wu suggests that our pursuit of excellence has infiltrated all aspects of our lives and corrupted the world of leisure. He believes that most people either don't have hobbies or don't find time to pursue them because we are afraid of being bad at them.

Even while relaxing and pursuing things with no short-term impact on our daily lives, the pursuit of excellence has become the hallmark of the 21st century. We aspire to be great partners, phenomenal lovers, inspiring co-workers and memorable party starters. Being mediocre, average or good enough doesn't feel quite right.

Research conducted at Harvard and INSEAD Business Schools suggests that happiness comes from progress. Excellence is an outcome of consistent progress, but the inverse is often not true. Unfortunately, the pursuit of excellence is far more in vogue than the pursuit of progress. This trickles down even to hobbies and leisure activities as we tend to link our identities and self-worth with them.

Leisure used to be part of our personal space, but it is far more public now. We track numbers, keep scores and measure relative progress. That is perhaps how leisure became hard work.

Angel List's co-founder, Naval Ravikant, shared, 'Find three hobbies: one that makes you fit, one that makes you money and one that makes you smart.' I found this three-pronged life hack immensely helpful but couldn't help wonder if hobbies need to have a goal attached to them.

There is abundant research that suggests that pursuing hobbies can make us better at our jobs. Shark Tank investor Kevin O'Leary pursues photography, film making and cooking, seriously. Wharton Professor Adam Grant suggests that hobbies train us to think creatively and give us access to new ways of solving problems. It turns out that Nobel-laureate scientists are twice as likely to play a musical instrument as their peers, and seven times as likely to paint or draw. Einstein described the theory of relativity as a musical thought and Galileo recognized the moon's mountains through a telescope because of his training in art. While it is clear that hobbies have practical benefits, I hope we don't indulge in them with an ulterior motive. Doing so will irreparably sully our creativity in the long run.

Let us explore the advantages and disadvantages of goal-driven, utilitarian approach to hobbies. The advantage is that we tend to pursue them more seriously and consistently put efforts even if just to prove a point. The disadvantage is that the joy of experience is replaced by the pressure of performance.

Right after high school, largely on a whim, I decided to take up theatre. Since then it has become an integral part of my life. Although I am a better theatre actor now, I cherish my first set of rehearsals, the evening chatter with other performers and the unmatched exhilaration of stepping on stage. At the time all I cared about was the sheer pleasure of pursuit. Today I hear my inner voice telling me to try and excel. I wonder if it is just me or we are all part of this hustle revolution together.

As Professor Wu explains, the demands of excellence—deliberate practise, coaching, competition—are at odds with freedom. If we only pursue hobbies and personal projects where we can excel, our field of exploration will reduce significantly. While we may fail fewer times, it will come at the cost of tinkering and experimentation. Eventually we might even stop learning new things because of risk of falling short of our expectations.

So how might we design our lives to leave room for wanton whims and hobbies? I feel it comes down to letting our curiosity shape our path ahead. Legislating curiosity can stifle innovation and personal growth. Most importantly, it can deprive us of the joy of discovering our true selves.

I still remember the summer I took to theatre. I didn't accomplish much and ended up with a small role in a local production, but it was one of the most defining summers I have ever had. Over the years, theatre has helped me in innumerable ways at work but that is not why I got into it. Perhaps that is why I got so much out of the experience.

Key Takeaways

- Happiness comes from progress.
- Pursuit of excellence is far more in vogue than the pursuit of progress.
- Leisure is no longer part of our personal space.
- Demands of excellence are at odds with the pursuit of freedom.
- Being utilitarian about our hobbies can backfire.

CHAPTER 11

IT IS TIME FOR PASSION ECONOMY

Coss Marte is the founder of Conbody, a prison style fitness bootcamp that hires ex-cons to teach fitness classes. Born to poor immigrant parents from Dominican Republic, Marte started dealing drugs in his teens and made more than USD 2 million a year before getting caught. He spent four years in prison where he discovered his passion for fitness and eventually figured out how to transform it into a viable profession. This kind of passion-centric job creation will drive the economic engine of the 21st century.

According to economist Adam Davidson and the recent *Future of Work* report published by venture capital firm Andreessen Horovitz, the gig economy and 'Uber for X' model will at least in part make way for passion economy where micro-entrepreneurs like Marte monetize their individuality and creativity.

Fitness centres are almost indistinguishable from each other. Business pundits call it an undifferentiated market with low barriers to entry and huge competition. Marte's fitness centres don't even have any equipment. They are basically small rooms with mirrors that Marte put up himself. He is an ex-con employing ex-cons offering a competitively priced fitness deal. Somehow 74 per cent of his customers never leave. The industry average is 25 per cent.

Marte's fitness classes are good and his subscription-based business model makes sense, but his success cannot be attributed to them. A key component of the passion economy is story-telling and Marte tells a gripping story through his business. It creates a strong bond between customers and instructors.

In addition to becoming fit, the customers are actually involved in the redemption of their instructors. Unlike other gyms where hourly paid instructors change every few months, Conbody instructors are there for life. Marte's genius is that he has taken objectively negative facets and found a way to tell a true story in an authentic way.

There are several other examples that demonstrate the power of story-telling in the passion economy. Dave Dahl spent 15 years in jail before setting up an organic bread company which he sold for USD 275 million in 2015. When I used to live in the United States, I would often have Dave's Killer Bread, not because of its taste (although it was very good) but because of the gripping story of the multi-million-dollar bread company set up by a young man trying to redeem himself.

Obviously, we do not need to go to jail to create a memorable story. The larger lesson is that some of the hardest, most painful aspects of our lives can become core pillars of our business strategy.

According to an investor at Andreessen Horovitz, Ji Lin, these stories are indicative of a larger trend called the 'enterprization of the consumer'. Whereas previously, gig economy flattened the individuality of workers, passion economy will allow anyone to monetize their unique skills or stories.

While the passion economy will be immensely rewarding for creators, it won't be all fun and games. People will need the discipline and the rigour to work hard, experiment fast and deliver consistently. Unlike regular employment, creators will need to figure out human resources (HR), accounting and legal issues themselves. Paul Jarvis, the author of *Company of One: Why Staying Small Is the*

Next Big Thing for Business, shares that today creators spend more than 50 per cent of their time doing extraneous stuff. That is a colossal waste of income and potential. I see a huge opportunity here.

Instead of debating whether AI will lead to job losses, we should figure out how it can augment the productivity of creators and micro-entrepreneurs. We need to free up time for creators to do the work they truly care about and are good at. That is how the passion economy will blossom and lead to the next wave of economic growth.

Will AI lead to job losses? Of course. Are the number of jobs in the world finite? Of course not. In the years to come, we will witness a reduction in the number of institutional jobs. Governments and enterprises will hire fewer people. Some jobs would even be outsourced to robots and algorithms.

This phase shift will be immensely stressful if we keep running after the next big thing or the next new technology without a sense of purpose. However, if we learn to augment our creative pursuits with meaningful stories and new age technologies, the passion economy will unleash innumerable possibilities, just like it did for Coss Marte and Dave Dahl.

Key Takeaways

- The gig economy will make way for the passion economy where people would monetize their unique life experiences and skills.
- Their underlying story will be the force multiplier of their business.
- We will witness the emergence of many companies of one.
- Being better will motivate people far more than being bigger in terms of scale and scope.

CHAPTER 12

WHEN SHOULD YOU QUIT YOUR JOB?

Few months before the publication of this book, I delivered a talk on the power of endings. Referencing academic research and case studies, I explained how endings influence most aspects of our lives—from election verdicts and vacation memories to Uber rides and divorce filings.

It turns out that endings also indicate when people are likely to leave their jobs. According to Daniel Pink's book *When*, the first-year anniversary is when most people quit. The second most likely? Their second-year anniversary. Third? Their third-year anniversary. Endings matter! Much more than we think.

Corporate Executive Board (CEB) delved deeper into the subject of employee attrition in a Harvard Business Review paper published in September 2016. The paper shows significant job-hunting spikes on work anniversaries, mid-life birthdays, and high school reunions.

Why is that? The end of an era or a momentous milestone nudges us to start afresh. The desire to reinvent is at its peak then. However, there is another reason. The CEB whitepaper concludes that people gauge their performance by comparing with peers, or with where they thought they would be at a certain point in life. Reunions catalyse this gentle envy into a strong call to action.

One of my main goals for writing this chapter is to provide a framework that helps millennials decide the right time to move on. This is important as my generation has often been accused of snacking on careers.

Someone asked Jack Ma about millennial's job hopping in Davos 2019. His reflections were noteworthy. He recommended that millennials stay in their jobs for at least three years, learn and then think about moving on. I believe the genesis of his view comes from personal experience.

Ma trained to become a high school teacher, something he had no interest in. He kept thinking that the day he graduates and completes the care minimum teaching requirements, he will move on to other things. On the day of graduation, his university president met him at the gate and asked him to stick it out in the school for six long years. Reluctantly, he agreed and kept the promise. Those six years calmed him down. He learned from his students and empowered them to be their best, a precious skill in a CEO.

Daniel Pink's analysis suggests that the ideal time to quit is either after three years of being in a job or five years from the date of joining. That's the timeframe when past experience is long enough to be considered relevant but not too long that the candidate is married to the company.

While research, and advice from stalwarts like Jack Ma has a lot of merit, it is important that we remember that the timeframes are suggestive, not prescriptive. It goes without saying that if the work environment is toxic and/or there is a mismatch of values, one should move on without batting an eyelid.

To write this chapter, I interviewed 26 millennials who had quit their jobs twice or more in 2020. Although the sample was small, it became abundantly clear that the dominant reason for quitting was bad fit or mismatched expectations. These millennials, many of who had impeccable academic records, were just not right for the job or the job turned out to be very different from the job description. I will point out that in some cases, the millennial timeframe for making impact seemed unreal. If you have been in a company for three months, you may not have the contextual understanding to propose mega structural changes. I know this because I made this mistake a few years back.

'Pick carefully, stick diligently' is my mantra for thinking about when to quit. I believe we should be careful with our choices, specially early on in our careers. If we choose sensibly, we are likely to have the motivation to follow through and not job hop on whims and micro-anxieties.

Life doesn't provide us enough time and energy to make everyone's career mistakes. That's why we have peer mentoring communities like Network Capital where millennials come together to learn with and from each other's professional experiences. I see our community members help each other make informed career decisions every day. Through the shared community experience, I have witnessed innumerable instances where members have nudged each other out of potentially disastrous career moves.

The rules of work and career are changing. It is acceptable and appropriate to quit if you're demotivated at work. Things might backfire, you might have to quit again and find something new. That's ok too, but consider Jack Ma's advice as you embark upon your next adventure.

Key Takeaways

- Take your time and do your research before starting a new job.
- Pick carefully, stick diligently. It takes a while to figure out the operating culture of workplaces.
- Statistically speaking, leaving after three years or five years is most advantageous.
- No matter what statistics say, don't stick around if there is a value mismatch.
- It is ok to quit but it isn't ok to quit every three months.

PART 2

BUILDING A TRIBE
OF MENTORS

CHAPTER 13

THE MENTORING PARADOX: NECESSARY BUT INSUFFICIENT

Despite solid gains in middle and senior management positions, women hold less than five per cent of Fortune 500 CEO seats. According to some studies like *The Sponsor Effect: Breaking Through the Last Glass Ceiling* and the more recent TED Talk by Wall Street Veteran, Carla Harris, it isn't a conspiracy but a surprising lack of advocacy from both men and women in positions of influence. What makes it complicated is that women have more mentors assigned to them than men—yet women are less likely to advance to leadership positions. In simple words, mentors help but mentorship is not enough.

Women and under-represented communities need sponsorship to march ahead. Let's try and understand the difference between mentorship and sponsorship.

Mentors understand our career aspirations and help us identify and think through key questions. They are catalysts for broadening our professional horizons, crafting a vision and expanding our networks. Most importantly, they help us track and measure our progress over time. No one can contest the role of mentors in shaping successful careers. In fact, it is hard to find even one person who excelled without a tribe of mentors. From Leonardo Da Vinci to Leo Tolstoy, mentors helped groom potential into performance.

That said, mentors have a limited role in pulling us up the next level. It is largely up to sponsors and how they bat for us.

Sponsors have three defining characteristics. First, they have a seat at the table where key career decisions are made. Second, they are familiar with your work and can vouch for your character. Third, they have influence.

It turns out that women have more than enough mentors but are only half as likely as their male peers to have a sponsor. Research shows that a large number of ambitious women underestimate the pivotal role sponsorship plays in their advancement. More importantly, the *Sponsor Effect* study pointed out that even women who do grasp the importance of relationship capital are unable to cultivate it effectively. Many feel that getting ahead based on 'who you know' is inherently unfair, even 'dirty'. This can be attributed in no small part to structural challenges, harassment and office gossip that women often have had to grapple with.

Sponsorship is far more than just knowing someone important. It is about cultivating a meaningful professional relationship on the basis of trust, performance and purpose. No matter what we feel about sponsorship, it is hard to contest that it matters.

According to Harvard Business Review, a sponsor confers a statistical career benefit of anything from 22 to 30 per cent, depending on what's being requested (assignment or pay raise) and who's asking (men or women). More than numbers, the presence of a sponsor can be a huge motivating factor, especially for professionals from under-represented communities and women returning to work after a hiatus. This is what a Network Capital community member said about her sponsor:

> I work at a large hedge fund in Hong Kong. My sponsor and I are the only two women on the floor. Although my firm offered great flexibility during my pregnancy, I was nervous coming back to office. I felt I owed everyone an explanation and tried overcompensating in ways that left me surprised.

Thankfully my sponsor noticed my less than normal behavior and took me out to lunch. As we were finishing up, she said that she had my back. That is when I knew that I could focus on my work without worrying much about perceptions.

Almost all organizations have mentoring programmes but very few have noteworthy results. These days reverse-mentoring and peer-mentoring programmes are fashionable. Some of them are well-intentioned and even yield promising results in the short term. But they are far from enough. Without sponsorship programmes and structures, mentoring initiatives fall flat.

Many organizations have now realized the importance of diversity and inclusion as key performance indicators. With thoughtful sponsorship schemes, we can ensure that the diverse talents being hired feel included and empowered to deliver their best every single day.

Setting up a transparent and accessible sponsorship programmes might not be easy but their tangible and intangible benefits far outweigh the short-term challenges.

To conclude, I would like to say that our tribe of mentors set us up for success but it is our sponsors who vouch for us behind closed doors where they have a voice and we don't have reach.

Key Takeaways

- Mentors help us figure out our career aspirations and think through key career questions.
- Sponsors have a seat at the table where practical career advancement decisions are taken.
- Women and minorities have very few sponsors.
- We need both mentors and sponsors to succeed.

CHAPTER 14

LEARN TO NETWORK THE PAUL ERDOS WAY

Paul Erdos was a quirky Jewish mathematician who could mentally calculate the number of seconds a person had lived at the age of four years. Time Magazine called him the Oddball's oddball. He was known for showing up at people's doors at odd hours saying, 'My mind is open.' This meant he was ready to take on new mathematical challenges.

Erdos wasn't the easiest of guests to host. He couldn't make his bed or boil water for his tea. He had very few clothes so the hosts were given the opportunity to do laundry for him. Legend has it that after a long night of brainstorming, when his collaborators (a mathematician couple) went to bed, he mischievously went to the kitchen and started throwing utensils around. Evidently, he had found a major breakthrough in the problem they were trying to solve. Despite such idiosyncratic behavior, it is a bit puzzling to note that Paul Erdos was probably the most loved, most networked and most talented mathematician.

The Fields Medal is the highest honour in mathematics. Erdos never won it, but several people he helped, did. Erdos is best known for the 'Erdos Number'. It wasn't a theorem or a tool, but a measure of how close you were to working with Paul Erdos. Research has shown that, in many cases, mathematical prowess is proportional to how closely you worked with/were influenced by Erdos. Two Nobel prize winners in physics have an Erdos Number of two. Fourteen have an Erdos Number of three. As Erik Barker puts it (drawing upon Adam Grant's research), Erdos made people great.

His collaboration principles were something we can all learn from—give serendipity a chance, be clear about your goal and focus on making the collaborator successful.

Let's delve deeper into each of them starting with the vital role of serendipity. Collaboration wasn't a transaction for Erdos. It was his language of expression. I am sure he never had an elevator pitch and I think you shouldn't either.

Simply changing the first few sentences in a conversation can have a disproportionate impact on the depth and breadth of discussions. We have become so used to app-induced efficiency that we have forgotten the art of building relationships—the core of collaboration. Yes, the strength of relationships is often a function of time but no matter how much time you give a relationship built entirely on utility, it is unlikely to blossom into something meaningful.

I realize that we are all pressed for time. A free-wheeling, exploratory conversation might be a luxury. So how do we build meaningful connections in the age of likes and swipes? I believe the answer lies in being intentional about the goal at hand and make the collaborator successful.

I can trace the origins of almost all my meaningful professional relationships to following this principle. The beauty is that it isn't dependent on seniority. Whether you are speaking to your CEO or your intern, s/he has challenges, goals and dilemmas. If you try and help, they value it. By following this principle, you are not only signalling your intent but also demonstrating your capability to perform complex tasks.

Paul Erdos was a difficult guest but people loved having him over. He would come over unannounced, whip up a storm, help unravel some mathematical mystery and leave for the next adventure without worrying about credits and footnotes.

What if we are a bit less strategic and a bit more Erdos while networking? No harm trying.

Key Takeaways

- Instead of thinking what you can get out of people, figure out how to add specific value to their lives.
- Give serendipity a chance, be clear about your goal and focus on making your collaborator successful.
- Don't treat conversations like transactions.
- Strategic networking tips are a waste of time.
- Be like Erdos.

CHAPTER 15

WHY YOU NEED A COACH AND A MENTOR

For the longest time, the best-kept secret of Silicon Valley wasn't a software or an incubator. It was a vivacious football coach turned sales guy called Bill Campbell. He went on weekly walks with Steve Jobs. The founders of Google said they wouldn't have made it without him. Such was the level of trust he inspired that both Google and Apple took Bill's counsel when they were going through the bitter dispute over some features of the Android operating system.

Bill didn't write a line of code or contribute to any product discussions. That's why it is a mystery how a non-technical football coach with a very average on-field track record transformed Silicon Valley and built companies that are collectively valued over trillion dollars.

In the year 2016, when Bill succumbed to cancer, Mark Zuckerberg, Larry Page, Sergey Brin, Jeff Besos and all major Silicon Valley stalwarts attended his funeral. He wasn't just respected, but also loved by everyone he ever worked with. He wasn't their mentor; he was their coach.

Bill inspired people to do great work, have a team-first approach and be their best selves every single day. People trusted him in good times and bad. When serial entrepreneur and investor,

Ben Horowitz had to fire an industry veteran, he reached out to Bill for advice. Bill said, 'You can't let him keep his job, but you absolutely can let him keep his respect.'

While mentors are essential for career growth, their role is restricted to sharing insights and ideas. They help us think things through but aren't really involved in implementing ideas. Coaches, on the other hand, roll up their sleeves and get their hands dirty. They empower us to see our blind spots, hold us accountable and take responsibility for making us better without taking credit for our accomplishments.

Let us understand how coaching came into sports and eventually permeated to all forms of management practice. In the year 1875, Harvard and Yale played one of the very first football games. Yale hired a head coach; Harvard did not. The results? Over the next three decades, Harvard won just four times. Then, Harvard hired a coach and the Yale–Harvard rivalry suddenly got more interesting. Many players from these sports teams went on to build successful careers in management and could trace their leadership development to early exposure to coaching.

Thanks to our innumerable biases and blind spots, we tend to be terrible judges of our growth and development. While we may get things right in broad strokes, we tend to ignore the micro elements that collectively compound to macro changes. Overnight progress is a myth and coaches help us realize that quickly.

If we want to master any skill, we need a coach. While we may not be lucky enough to have Bill Campbell in flesh and blood, we do have his principles. My favourite 'Billism' is: Always build communities. Everyone has something to learn and something to share. Being part of and adding value to our communities is the most effective way to learn and find someone to learn with.

As part of the Network Capital learning community, we recently piloted peer coaches. These are fellow community members who help their peers with the power of objective feedback. It is entirely voluntary, but the initial results have been promising. Peer coaches are helping each other increase GMAT scores, enabling more efficient interview preparation, encouraging reading with higher focus, and writing better, among other things.

In addition to tangible improvements in skills, the community effect serves as a huge force multiplier. Our members push each other to achieve more because they know that there is someone in the same community looking out for them.

In modern workplaces, managers should ideally serve as coaches. Their job is not to police progress and give performance rankings but to inspire their teammates to be their best. They need to create psychological safety within their team so that the team moves together in one direction with the right attitude, commitment and skills. This is of course easier said than done. That's why Bill Campbell always said, 'Only coach the coachable.'

Key Takeaways

- Coaches empower us to see our blind spots, hold us accountable and empower us to get better.
- You need mentors, sponsors and coaches.
- Find a coach and be one to someone in need. Peer coaching is a vital tool for professional growth.
- Managers should coach, not police employees.

CHAPTER 16

WHY WEAK TIES MAKE A STRONG NETWORK

In the year 1973, a Professor at Stanford, Mark Granovetter, published a seminal paper titled *The Strength of Weak Ties*. Granovetter categorized interpersonal ties as strong, weak or absent. In simple words, strong ties are friends and weak ties are acquaintances.

Weak ties are important for two reasons. First, we are more likely to articulate what we need to an acquaintance. This might be counter-intuitive but when we speak with friends, we tend to skip contextual details and largely rely on implicit communication. However, when we communicate with acquaintances, we are forced to explicitly state what we want and why.

The second reason why weak ties matter is that they exponentially increase one's network. Based on in-depth interviews of 100 white-collar workers who had switched jobs in the last five years, Granovetter discovered that weak ties helped most of them find their next job.

Before jumping to conclusions, it is important to keep in mind that the study was conducted in 1973. That was the time when social and professional networking happened almost entirely offline. Back then, weak ties were disproportionately important as access to information was a challenge. Today, however, technology has changed the game. Information is still network dependent but to a lesser extent.

University of Chicago's *Journal of Labor Economics* published a paper in 2017 analysing employment data from Facebook. Using anonymized, aggregated US data based on employment dates published by six million people on their Facebook profiles, researchers came to two conclusions: Most people still find their jobs through their numerous weak ties and an individual strong tie is more likely to help than an individual weak tie.

I see this in action every day on Network Capital. Hundreds of millennials float their *curriculum vitae's* (CV) and seek guidance for jobs and internships from a global community of peer mentors they don't know. This broadens their opportunity pool to include more than just their social networks, thereby creating contexts for meaningful opportunities to manifest.

However, I have noticed that the most successful job seekers take an additional step, in line with the findings of *Journal of Labor Economics*. They complement their posting on meta networks by reaching out to and reconnecting with specific people, especially old classmates, ex-colleagues, former bosses and clients. These sets of people were not just weak ties or acquaintances. They could talk knowledgeably and convincingly about the applicant's capabilities.

The altered technology and media ecology from the 1970s to today has created wider awareness about the presence of jobs. Many more people apply for the same set of opportunities, thereby further complicating the challenge of standing out from the pack. That is where a recommendation from a strong tie, especially someone who can vouch for your skills, comes handy. At the very least, such a referral will get you a foot within the door.

There are many ways to engineer one's social network to create an optimum mix of strong and weak ties but using algorithms to keep in touch can become tedious and disingenuous over a period of time. A much more effective way is to add value to your network regularly.

For your strong ties, you could consider sharing details of your work life beyond colourful social media snippets, seek and provide feedback or recommend them for appropriate opportunities. For your weak ties, you could make introductions, organize community events or drop an unexpected mail. These are some ways that work for me. You must discover your own ways of adding value.

Just remember the rule of thumb: If adding value to your strong and weak ties becomes too much work, you are probably not doing it right. Common reasons include networking fatigue, burnout and boredom.

I can trace the origin of every job I have had to a serendipitous context created by my strong and weak ties. Towards the end of business school, I met with an accident and missed the opportunity to appear for all final round recruitment interviews. The next few months were challenging as I wasn't sure how to restart the job hunt.

That's when, out of nowhere, an adjunct professor working at a large technology company replied to an email I had sent him six months back. It was a simple thank you note with a short analysis of the problem he discussed. Evidently, he liked my thought process and asked me if I was free for a call to dive deeper.

Two days later, we got on a call and at the end of it, he asked me to apply for an open position in his team. Five interview rounds and six weeks later, I got the job and started afresh with renewed belief in the power of serendipity and the importance of meaningful ties.

Key Takeaways

- Weak ties are sources of new information and insights.
- You need to leverage both your strong and weak networks and figure out ways to add value to both.
- If adding value to your strong and weak ties becomes too much work, you are probably not doing it right.

CHAPTER 17

PARADOX OF TRUST: TALKING TO STRANGERS

Amanda Knox was an American studying in Italy who was falsely accused and convicted of murdering her roommate. She ended up spending six years in prison before being released. Her only crime was not appearing sad enough in the middle of a murder investigation. Now consider Bernie Madoff, who seemed both trustworthy and reassuring, even while he ran the world's largest ponzi scheme. Citing such examples, Malcolm Gladwell explains why we make colossal judgement errors in his new book *Talking to Strangers*.

We are constantly interacting with people whom we don't know well and our psychological clumsiness, preconceived notions and over-reliance on gut leads to misunderstandings at work, in social situations and even on social media. Few years back, University of Alabama's Professor Timothy Levine's developed the truth-default theory that suggests that given the choice to believe a stranger or not, almost all of us choose to believe, to trust, to give the benefit of the doubt. This holds true for FBI agents, judges and intelligence specialists despite their rigorous training.

If we are too naively unquestioning, should we compensate with a healthy dose of paranoia and scepticism in our daily lives? Absolutely not. Doing so will bring the entire economy to a halt. Oxford researcher, Rachel Botsman, suggests that almost all technology-led productivity gains are enabled by leaps of trust. We travel, date, rent, work and live with people we know almost nothing about. Imagine life without Uber, Airbnb and other platform economy wonders!

Research by Pew Research Center suggests that people are trusting governments and big institutions like banks and religious organizations much less than they used to. In fact, institutional trust is at an all-time low and is making way for peer-to-peer trust which is far more accessible and approachable.

I see this in action every day on Network Capital where millennials around the world seek mentoring and career advice from peers. They are often strangers to begin with but the process of helping each other build meaningful careers creates a strong bond that often leads to new, mutually beneficial opportunities over time.

Can things go awry when we trust strangers? Absolutely. As Gladwell's book suggests, we often pay a price for our naivete but at a macro-level, the advantages of giving strangers the benefit of doubt are greater than the price we pay when trusting them backfires.

One person who did not subscribe to Levine's 'Truth Default' theory was an independent fraud investigator named Harry Markopolos, who tried to get the authorities to investigate Madoff on numerous occasions. He was so distrusting of everyone that when he had an opportunity to meet with a prosecutor to discuss Madoff's case, he chose to leave the information anonymously. He was convinced that both Madoff and the government were out there to get him and he spent months on end without proper sleep, hiding under his bed. Gladwell says that if everyone on Wall Street behaved like Harry Markopolos, there would be no fraud on Wall Street but the air would be so thick with suspicion and paranoia that there would also be no Wall Street at all.

A useful mental model to deal with strangers is Hanlon's Razor theory which suggests that we should never attribute to malice what can be explained by carelessness or stupidity. This is especially important in the digitally connected world where we text more than we meet, date people in different time zones and incessantly tweet about productivity and politics. Judgement errors and misunderstandings are bound to happen but we can avoid the side effects if we train ourselves to give the benefit of doubt to strangers, as Hanlon's Razor theory prescribes.

Subconsciously we expect strangers to be transparent and reveal their thoughts in their demeanour, body language and actions. But they don't—not reliably. People who are nervous and sweaty and otherwise guilty looking—like Amanda Knox—are just as likely to be telling the truth as they are to be lying. And the cool and collected ones—like Bernie Madoff—may simply be good at the confidence game.

Gladwell has a simple formula for dealing with strangers, an adaptation of Hanlon's Razor: Trust people with caution and humility. Caution because things can backfire and humility because we are not particularly good at reading strangers.

Key takeaways

- Don't trust unquestioningly.
- Be careful not to make error judgements when it comes to reading strangers.
- Almost all human progress has been a result of the trust leaps we take every day.
- The advantages of giving strangers the benefit of doubt are greater than the price we pay when trusting them backfires.
- Trust strangers with caution and humility.

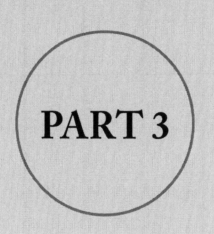

PART 3

NAVIGATING
THE MODERN
WORKPLACE:
MILLENNIAL
MATTERS

CHAPTER 18

MILLENNIAL'S SEARCH FOR MEANING

Being a millennial is hard work. In the era of dizzying disruptions, we are expected to change the world and find happiness in doing so. The happiness industry is buzzing. In the early nineties, there were a few hundred studies about happiness published each year. By the year 2014, the number had jumped to 10,000. Since the mid-2000s, the interest in happiness, as measured by Google searches, has trebled. Who do you think is searching happiness most fervently? Will it surprise you if it were the freshly minted graduates joining the work force?

Unfortunately, the obsession with happiness has failed to deliver on its promise. There is growing body of research such as the one conducted by Aekyoung Kim of Rutgers University and Sam Maglio of the University of Toronto that explains how the constant pursuit of happiness can ironically undermine well-being. The duo found that people obsessed with happiness often feel like they do not have enough time in the day, and this paradoxically makes them feel unhappy. Since time is the key analysis parameter of this research, the findings are most relevant to the millennials, the generation that managed to overwork itself into burnouts, thereby inventing the phrase, 'quarter life crisis'.

To get real-time feedback, I conducted a survey on Network Capital. It turns out that 85 per cent of the respondents (mostly millennials), believed that their pursuit of happiness was making them unhappy. Given the body of research and survey findings, is there any hope?

I believe there is, and the first step is to stop trying to be happy all the time. We need to let go of the pressure to be happy and repivot to finding meaning. According to Viktor E. Frankl, holocaust survivor and founder of Logotherapy, the true meaning of life is discovered in the world rather than within one's psyche. This implies that we need to create contexts for people to discover their reason for being. Given that millennials spend more than half their lives at work, companies have a critical role in helping discover their potential and find meaning. Let's explore if that's happening today.

According to the Gallup US study *How Millennials Want to Work and Live*, millennials struggle to find good jobs that engage them. They have the highest rates of unemployment and underemployment, and only 29 per cent of employed millennials are engaged at work. Half of the millennials say they feel good about the amount of money they have to spend, and less than 40 per cent are what Gallup defines as 'thriving' in any aspect of well-being. Therefore, it is safe to say that most workplaces are taking meaning out of the lives of millennials. That said, all isn't lost. With conscious effort from both millennials and their employers, we can overcome this pervasive crisis.

As author, Emily Esfahani Smith eloquently puts it, there are four pillars of meaning: belonging, purpose, transcendence and storytelling (the story we tell ourselves). Employers are vital for the first pillar–belonging. They can create contexts for millennials to work with and add value to different communities/teams within the company. I have found cross-functional projects where senior management has skin in the game to be catalysts in increasing sense of belonging.

For pillars two, three and four, the onus is largely on the millennials. It all begins by realizing that true meaning isn't found in success and glamour but the mundane. This is especially important for us to keep in mind as we are living in the times of likes, swipes, filters and fads. According to the American Psychology Association's research paper published in 2015 by University of California, Los Angeles (UCLA), University of Illinois at Urbana-Champaign (UIUC) and Arizona State University Professors, adolescents who did household chores felt a stronger sense of purpose as they believed they were contributing to something bigger—their families.

During a visit to the NASA space centre in 1962, President John F. Kennedy noticed a janitor carrying a broom. He interrupted his tour, walked over to the man and said, 'Hi, I'm Jack Kennedy. What are you doing?'

'Well, Mr President,' the janitor responded, 'I'm helping put a man on the moon.'

Zooming out from Kennedy in NASA to your own office today: If you see someone crunching numbers quietly in a corner on a Friday evening, acknowledge them and ask—what are you doing? You might be surprised by what you hear.

Key Takeaways

- Constant pursuit of happiness can ironically undermine well-being.
- We need to repivot the search for happiness into the quest for meaning.
- There are four pillars of meaning: belonging, purpose, transcendence and storytelling (the story we tell ourselves).
- With consistent efforts, keeping the four pillars of meaning in mind, we can overcome the pervasive deficit of meaning.

CHAPTER 19

TYRANNY OF JOB DESCRIPTIONS

Almost all job descriptions are impersonal, boring, wordy and vague. They make the most interesting work opportunities sound like a long list of chores. Although most companies parrot the virtues of diversity and thinking out of the box, they tend to attract people who neatly fit conventional norms of performance. Round pegs in square holes are great for advertisements but how often do you see them at work?

On average, job descriptions tend to be about 700 words, roughly the length of this chapter. They pontificate on buzz words like team work, collaboration and communication before quickly jumping ship to past experiences and academic qualifications. Therein lies a major flaw. They expect past performance to be an accurate indicator of future potential. I have rarely come across a job description that gives a flavour of what it takes to do a job well.

We live in an era of unprecedented disruption. What worked in the past may not work in the future. Variability and uncertainty are expected to be operating conditions of the 21st century. Organizations need people who can think on their feet, learn from failures and keep an open mind for the future. Job descriptions do a great job of keeping such people away, especially if they happen to be women or minorities.

I graduated from business school over five years ago. In this period, the nature of work has changed, global political context has evolved, multi-billion dollar companies have been burnt and built, scientific research has become much more mainstreamed, 100 per cent vegetarian beef burgers have been created, national constitutions have been amended, but somehow, job descriptions have remained the same.

Is it a conspiracy or intellectual lethargy? Probably both. The intellectual lethargy can be ascribed to laziness but the conspiracy is more interesting to analyse. While we can explore this from various angles, let us dive deep into the gender aspect of job search and how job descriptions play a villainous role.

According to an internal report published by Hewlett Packard, men apply for jobs when they meet only 60 per cent of the qualifications, but women apply only if they meet 100 per cent of the qualifications.

Author Tara Mohr has analysed this gender differential in detail. According to her research, almost 78 per cent of women's reasons for not applying come from assuming that job qualifications are real requirements to get hired and do the job well. They believe that the hiring process is far more by the book than it really is. Ms Mohr believes that there are three reasons for this—primary schooling, hiring norms and modern history. Let's explore each of them.

First, girls are strongly socialized to—follow the rules—from primary school and are rewarded for doing so. While following rules works for academic grades, when it comes to applying for jobs, this habit tends to backfire. Second, men are often hired and promoted for potential, women, for their prior experience and track record. Witnessing this in their workplaces makes women less likely to apply to jobs that aren't a perfect match for their qualifications. Third, women were able to break into the workforce in the 20th century only if they had the right accreditations.

Not much has changed today. Both job descriptions and mindsets remain firmly rooted in the past.

Additional research commissioned by the German Ministry of Education concluded that language also plays a key role in deterring women. It was deduced that when women find job descriptions sprinkled with words like 'assertive', 'independent', 'aggressive', they are less likely to apply. Conversely, if the job descriptions use words like 'dedicated', 'responsible', 'conscientious' and 'sociable', they are much more likely to think that the job is a good fit. Even simple language tweaks can have a huge impact but organizations need to stop playing by the already rigged book.

Enabling diversity at work is a challenge that can't be solved through tokenisms like colourful posters, motivational videos and omnipresent diversity days.

It is time to hold companies and institutions accountable to what they preach. Job descriptions are the first point of communication with potential applicants. If companies really care about attracting diverse candidates, they should humanize job descriptions and incentivize candidates from all walks of life to apply instead of mechanically inserting 'equal opportunity employer' towards the end of the page.

Key Takeaways

- Most job descriptions are wordy and vague.
- Jobs have changed drastically but job descriptions remain the same.
- Job descriptions can perpetuate biases.
- Subtle changes in the language, and efforts to humanize job descriptions can help overcome access challenge.
- It is time to hold companies accountable to what they preach.

CHAPTER 20

THE PUZZLE OF GREAT EXPECTATIONS

Daniel Kish is a handsome 53 years old adventurer who lost his eyes to cancer as a toddler. He is also the president of *The World Access for the Blind*, a California based non-profit organization with a mission to spread awareness about the strengths and capabilities of people with all forms of blindness.

Four years ago, he guided National Public Radio (NPR) host Lulu Miller on a hike deep into the woods. Daniel even rides a bike. He does this using a technique called echolocation. Much like bats, he clicks with his tongue to understand his geospatial position. From the way those clicks bounce off, Daniel gets a sonic representation of surrounding objects. He has trained himself to see despite being blind and is quite literally, Batman.

Daniel believes that most blind people who don't have other disabilities could do things like ride bikes. It isn't clicking or under-developed echolocation techniques but society's low expectations that come in the way. Thankfully, Daniel's mother chose a different approach.

Paulette Kish let him rise, fall, learn and try again. She expected him to overcome odds and rise to his potential. It worked. From

5th grade, Daniel walked to school every day, crossed major streets and made his own breakfast.

The powerful influence of one person's expectations on another's behaviour has long been recognized by physicians, behavioural scientists and teachers. Carol Dweck's (Lewis and Virginia Eaton Professor of Psychology at Stanford University) paper *Academic Tenacity* explained how teachers' expectations can raise or lower a student's IQ; mother's expectations can affect drinking behaviour of her middle schooler; and military trainers' expectations can make a cadet faster or slower. According to research published by the United States National Library of Medicine, even in romantic relationships, higher expected future satisfaction correlates with stronger commitment. At work, your manager's expectations can influence both you and your team's performance. We behave differently with people we expect less from. The signs are subtle but observable. We tend to adopt a different tone, avoid eye contact and stand further away.

The empirical evidence about expectations seems counter-intuitive. On Network Capital, I conducted a survey asking millennials if they thought high expectations translated to better performance. Seventy per cent disagreed. Many of our community members commented that high expectations put additional pressure and cause performance anxiety.

To put things in perspective, let us refer to research by a professor at the University of Michigan, John W. Atkinson. He demonstrated that the relationship between motivation to succeed and expectancy varies in the form of a bell-shaped curve. The degree of motivation and effort rises until the success probability is 50 per cent, then begins to fall even though the expectancy of success continues to increase. Simply setting impossible goals and expecting more can backfire. That is why it is important to progressively calibrate both expectations and effort, just like Paulette Kish.

Effective managers and coaches tend to create high performance expectations that their team members consistently fulfil. How do they do that? Academician J. Sterling Livingston believes that the difference lies in their confidence to develop talent. What comes as a surprise is that high expectations of such managers are based primarily on what they think about themselves. Their self-belief impacts what they expect of their subordinates, and how they treat them. This seems to be true in Daniel and his mother-cum-coach Paulette Kish's case.

Paulette Kish had a tough marriage. After many years of feeling small and powerless, she vowed that she would never be ruled by fear again. Her expectation of her renewed self, helped shape her expectation of her son, Daniel. She believed that despite the physical challenges, Daniel would grow up to be a great man. And he did.

Closer home, a friend and fellow Network Capital community member, Gaurav, has a precarious eye condition. Gaurav has pro-gressively been losing vision to the extent that he can barely see anything today. He is the promoter of a large education company, an investor and a prolific speaker. Recently Network Capital's community manager requested him to conduct a live masterclass on stoicism for thousands of millennials. There were quite a few logistical constraints, but she knew it would turn out great. Strong preparation coupled with her high expectations propelled Gaurav to deliver one of the most viewed masterclasses on Network Capital TV (networkcapital.tv).

Expectations have the power to transform potential into perfor-mance. That's why next time you feel like giving up on someone, think harder.

Key Takeaways

- Expectations transform potential to performance.
- We behave differently with people we expect less from. We adopt a different tone, avoid eye contact and stand further away.
- Relationship between motivation to succeed and expectancy varies in the form of a bell-shaped curve.
- Talent isn't fixed. Some of the most successful coaches and managers have the confidence to develop talent.

CHAPTER 21

WHY MOONSHOTS MATTER

On a hot summer afternoon in the year 1962, in the middle of the Cold War, President John F. Kennedy delivered a historic address at Rice University. He called on his nation to commit to landing a human on the moon and returning him safely before the end of the decade. 'We choose to go to the moon in this decade and do the other things, not because they are easy but because they are hard,' Kennedy thundered, speaking before a packed audience comprising students, distinguished scientists and policy makers.

Although President Kennedy's Rice University address is more popular, the speech that positioned America to win the space race was delivered in Congress one year before President Kennedy's address. History would have taken a very different course if Lyndon Johnson (LBJ), the Vice President at the time, had not altered Kennedy's plan. Kennedy wanted to focus on military competition with the Soviet Union and have a clerk read out a page on the lunar mission. It was LBJ who convinced him otherwise.

Next day all national newspapers covered his speech. The leading story wasn't the cold war. It was the lunar mission. That's when Kennedy truly committed to the cause and immersed himself in making it happen.

His speech in Congress galvanized the media and united the American public. Both Republicans and Democrats lent their support to the mission. This was a spectacular achievement considering the fact that Kennedy was addressing the Congress right after Bay of Pigs, the failed military invasion of Cuba undertaken by the Central Intelligence Agency (CIA). It had become a massive global embarrassment and Kennedy had a lot on the line.

The year 1961 was also a time of deep social, political and economic crisis in America. Soviet Union was ahead on several parameters, especially space technology. They had already sent a man to space. Despite that, Kennedy convinced the American people to channel their tax dollars to the intensely expensive—almost equivalent to USD 200 billion today—space adventure with no short-term economic benefits.

There are five key lessons to be learned from Kennedy's leadership style. First, SMART (specific, measurable, attainable, relevant and time-bound) goals matter. As author, Tim Ferris puts it, life punishes the vague wish and rewards the specific ask. Even while explaining a high-risk project with myriad uncertainties, Kennedy clearly defined timelines, success parameters and next steps. He was inspiring because he was specific and his specificity gave credibility to the goal he outlined. Second, meaningful mission statements that touch upon something larger than our own selves have the power to transform a distant dream into a realistic outcome. Kennedy made the moonshot—a term that became popular after his speech—seem realistic not only to engineers and scientists but also to the public at large. Third, courageous leadership thrives in turbulent times. Adversity brings out the best in leaders. Kennedy rose to the occasion when the chips were down. He lifted the spirit of the entire nation and channelled individual despair into collective hope. Fourth, we can make healthy competition and even rivalry work for us. Eight years between President Kennedy's address and the actual moon landing, America saw an exponential increase in innovation and creativity. It was Kennedy's genius to leverage the rivalry with Soviet Union and further strengthen the American innovation muscle. Fifth, moonshots need radical collaboration at scale. Although President Kennedy was a key figure, the actual moon landing was a result of collaboration among thousands of engineers, budgetary legwork by LBJ and riveting storytelling and salesmanship by James Webb, the then head of NASA.

The next giant leap will probably be the Mars landing, but it was Apollo 11 that made space real for all of us. 20 July 2019 was the 50th anniversary of National Moon Day. In a poetic gesture that exemplifies humility unknown in the 21st century, Michael Collins, one of the three Astronauts of Apollo 11 who stayed back to monitor the space shuttle, tweeted, 'They did it, President Kennedy's dream come true, as thrilling today as it was 50 years ago.'

Sure, we need more Kennedys, but we also need more Collins—those who do their jobs with dignity without worrying about who gets the credit.

Key Takeaways

- Life punishes the vague wish and rewards the specific ask.
- Meaningful mission statements that touch upon something larger than our own selves have the power to transform a distant dream into a realistic outcome.
- Courageous leadership thrives in turbulent times.
- Moonshots need radical collaboration at scale.

CHAPTER 22

WHAT SOCIAL MOVEMENTS AND WORKPLACES CAN LEARN FROM EACH OTHER

Bang in the middle of city-wide protests of the year 2019, I found myself in Hong Kong. Even at the airport, there were unmissable signs of peaceful unrest. Surprisingly, there was no disruption of public services and I reached Kennedy Town in thirty minutes flat. Hong Kong managed to be efficient even while protesting!

Over the course of a long, meandering dinner with local Network Capital community members, I learned subtle nuances of what was going on in Hong Kong and realized how much start-ups and social movements have in common. In fact, they can learn a lot from each other.

Social movements are loosely connected small groups that are united by a shared purpose. This shared purpose is what start-up founders call mission statements, founding pillars of their company. Belief in the mission statement inspires collective action and unites different teams to work towards a common cause. For start-ups, that common cause is market leadership and for social movements it is structural change.

Like start-ups, most social movements and protests fail. Srđa Popović, Serbian political activist and author of *Blueprint for Revolution: How to Use Rice Pudding, Lego Men, and Other*

Non-Violent Techniques to Galvanize Communities, Overthrow Dictators, or Simply Change the World, offers a five-pronged strategy to create successful social movements. His strategy also has important lessons for start-up founders chasing ambitious moonshots.

First, define the change you want to see. You can oppose as many things as you like but unless you make an affirmative case and define exactly what you want, nothing will get done. Mahatma Gandhi wanted freedom from the British, women's suffrage movement wanted equal voting rights, India's pride movement wanted Section 377 of the Indian Penal Code, 1861 to be repealed and Serbia's Bulldozer Revolution wanted the dictator Slobodan Milošević to be removed. The start-up analogy is that founders are bound to fail if they don't define where they want their company to be in a stipulated time period. This is especially true if your company is in trouble and facing competitive threats. There is no substitute for clarity of purpose.

Second, shift the spectrum of allies. Popović explains that successful movements don't overpower their opponents; they gradually undermine their opposition's support. Extrapolating this learning to start-ups, you are unlikely to bamboozle your competition with brute force. If the competition is worthy, you will need to win one customer and one partner at a time, slowly eroding your competitor's arsenal. Once you win a critical mass of customers and partners, word will spread and the odds of victory will tilt in your favour.

Third, identify the pillars of power. Popular support is necessary but insufficient to succeed. Without institutional support, movements are bound to fail. In Serbia, Popovic's revolutionary group *Otpor* saw arrests of their members as an opportunity to strengthen relations with the police. The protesters were trained to defend officers placed in volatile areas. That's why when the police had to decide whether to shoot into crowds or join *Otpor,* they chose the latter. This is precious advice for start-ups, especially ones that get strong initial traction. Social media affirmation helps but does not automatically translate to increased revenue or market share. In order to reach their true potential, they need institutional support from government, press and media, partners or investors.

Fourth, seek to attract, not to overpower. This is particularly important for voters, customers and protestors who are undecided and fall in the middle of our spectrum of allies. You can only bring them to your side with relatable examples and stories that gently make a point. As Nobel Laureate Richard Thaler explains, a nudge is stronger than threat.

Fifth, construct a plan to survive victory. Remember what happened after Arab Spring? After a round of secular protests, the Muslim Brotherhood won the elections and came to power. Both start-ups and social movements need to build follow-up plans after achieving critical milestones. A fresh round of funding doesn't mean that you have arrived. It only means that you need to recalibrate your goals and figure out a way to achieve them. That's the time to strengthen relationships with your customers and partners. Many high growth start-ups forget the basics and get carried away with affirmations from media.

After Zoom's initial public offering (IPO), its founder, Eric Yuan, said that an IPO is like graduating from high school where we celebrate for a day keeping in mind that we don't want high school to be the peak of our performance. Keeping Yuan's advice and Popović's five principles in mind is essential for all start-up founders and leaders of social movements who believe in playing the long game.

Key Takeaways

- Social movements can teach important management lessons to start-ups.
- Be clear about the change you wish to see.
- Gradually shift the spectrum. Instant change doesn't work.
- Identify key pillars of power.
- Attraction is stronger than brute force.
- Play the long game.

CHAPTER 23

THE IKEA EFFECT

My first business school project was to build a wooden bridge for a global non-profit organization that could help kids with disabilities. It was a particularly cold day sprinkled with bouts of snow and rain. I was feverish, jet-lagged, under-dressed and famished after a long flight. By the time I reached my apartment, it was almost morning, time to head to school.

I was definitely not ready for intense physical activity. However, with support from my group mates, I powered through. Together, we tinkered through the day and built the bridge. Although it was crooked at the edges, it seemed sturdy. A team of structural engineers evaluated our bridge and concluded that it was strong enough. Children from the non-profit would actually use it.

We felt satisfied with what we had done. Somehow all the hours spent tinkering in the snow felt worth it.

This DIY (do-it-yourself) approach is becoming increasingly popular around the world. From corporate retreats to romantic getaways, astute programme designers ensure a DIY component in their itinerary. The DIY approach works because it makes us appreciate the labour of love. It adds more meaning to our experience and creates memorable stories. However, there is another reason—the IKEA effect. Named after the global furniture company, IKEA effect states that consumers place a disproportionately high value on products they create.

A Professor of psychology at Duke University, Dan Ariely collaborated with two Harvard professors and studied people assembling IKEA boxes, folding Origami and assembling Lego sets. They brought participants into the lab, and either gave them a pre-assembled LEGO car, or LEGOs and instructions to build the car. Then they asked the volunteers how much would they be willing to pay to keep their car? It turns out the participants were willing to pay twice as much for the LEGO car if they just finished building it. IKEA effect is particularly strong after successful completion of tasks.

We value things we build ourselves, but that's intuitive. Is there more to it?

Research shows that people who share the same birthday are slightly more likely to get married to one another. People named Carpenter are more likely to *be* carpenters and those with the last name Baker are more likely to be bakers. There's at least a modest tendency for women named Georgia to gravitate towards Georgia, women named Virginia to gravitate towards Virginia, and the more closely the name resembles the state, the bigger the effect appears to be. This can be attributed to implicit egotism, a term coined by Dr Brett Pelham from Montgomery University, that suggests we have an unconscious preference for things we relate to.

At work, we can sometimes commit to our own ideas even if they aren't the best. The 'Not Invented Here' syndrome refers to the popularly observed bias where managers refuse to use perfectly good ideas developed elsewhere in favour of their—sometimes inferior—internally-developed ideas. Studies demonstrate that when managers persist in pursuing failed projects and concepts, they do so because they truly come to believe their ideas are precious.

The combined might of IKEA effect, implicit egotism and 'Not Invented Here' syndrome makes effective decision-making tricky. Does that mean we ignore our convictions because they might be biased?

I subscribe to technology forecaster, Paul Saffo's decision making framework called 'Strong Opinions, Weakly Held'. Paul suggests that despite lack of available information, we should develop a strong, fact-based hypothesis. Conviction is an important decision-making tool, but it shouldn't blind us. We should continually gather information that either supports or refutes our hypothesis. If we uncover information unfriendly to our belief, we should abandon our belief. That doesn't make us flaky. If anything, it shows maturity. Clinging to our idea in the face of contradictory information is the origin of most bad decisions.

I missed sharing a small yet important aspect of my first business school project. We were a team of five people and I was the only mechanical engineer. I was experienced and had built several similar structures in college. However, my past experiences were misguiding me. I had failed to account for difference of material and tools. Had we gone ahead with the strategy I proposed initially, the bridge would not be stable. Thankfully, other members of my group chimed in and helped build a robust bridge. Together we completed the task in record time and thoroughly enjoyed the process.

Unknowingly, I was following Paul Saffo's 'Strong Opinions, Weakly Held' framework. It served me well then and continues to do so today.

Key Takeaways

- We place a disproportionately high value on products we create ourselves.
- Conviction in our own ideas is an important decision-making tool but it shouldn't blind us.
- It is ok to change our minds if evidence does not support our hypothesis.
- History sometimes teaches us the wrong lesson.
- Have strong opinions that are weakly held.

CHAPTER 24

AN ODE TO ENVY

Recently I was invited to speak at a Swedish conference on cross-border innovation. The evening kicked off on a tantalizing note, with drones presenting the summit report to all participants. Armed with meticulous notes on knowledge transfer, skill sharing and research investments, I felt prepared, yet jaded. Something was clearly amiss.

Having attended umpteen technology conclaves, I didn't want to do the obvious—extol the virtues of disruption or paint a dystopian vision of the future. That's why I decided to talk about a formidable, colourful and mysterious force that transcends boundaries: envy. Among other things, envy contributes to innovation and shapes human behaviour at work and play.

Simply put, envy is secret admiration. It is an unintended compliment that cracks us open and reveals things we truly value. Fredrick Nietzsche called envy and jealousy private parts of the human soul; Socrates said envy was the ulcer of the soul; and Aristotle went to the extent of stating that envy was the pain caused by the good fortune of others.

It is hard to understand the gaze of envy, but British psychologist Richard Smith offers two guiding parameters—relevance and similarity.

We tend to envy people whose work is similar to ours and those who are comparable to us. Even if we work in the technology industry, Steve Jobs and Bill Gates are unlikely to be objects of our envy; they inspire us. It is more probable that we are a tad envious of that perky colleague who built the tool everyone is raving about. Does envy make us human?

Let's first explore the two categories of envy: malignant and benign. Both are deeply personal and involve comparing ourselves to people we perceive are better off. However, with malicious envy, our focus is on wishing that the object of our envy didn't have the structural, cultural or positional advantages we wish we had. Germans have a word for it: *schadenfreude*.

Benign envy is more innocent. It focuses on the object of our envy but only to figure out ways to emulate it. People we benignly envy are a lot like us. We constantly think that with a little more luck and effort, we could become like them or even better.

While it may sound like admiration, benign envy is an exhausting full-time job that never celebrates a Sunday. That said, it can also be a self-help tool that spurs competition and sparks innovation. Since the Cricket World Cup, 2019, was being played during the time I was writing this chapter, let's explore this from the world of cricket. Cricket is an open skill sport, where the environment is constantly changing.

Research by Japanese professors Atsushi Oshio, Yuki Ueno and Satoshi Suyama suggests the level of competition is positively correlated with benign envy in open skill sports. In other words, benign envy helps closely matched cricketers compete harder and find new ways to get better. Almost all cricketing rivalries can partially be attributed to benign envy. Many fast bowlers, often from the same team, have publicly spoken about the positive influence of their beloved rival in upping their game.

Envy is a great equalizer. Whether you are a saint, a sinner, or somewhere in between, you cannot escape the occasional gaze of envy. Envy is omnipresent. Envy is involuntary. While we can't choose how we feel, we have control over how we manage it.

Next time your intern or someone you manage does something that inspires you, yet leaves you questioning your relevance, remember it is perhaps nothing more than a mood swing of benign envy. You can use it as motivation to be your best self.

The future of work is all about radical collaboration. In large teams, jealousy and envy are inevitable. Channel this individualistic benign envy into the collective growth of the organization.

The Pali language has a term, *mudita*, which roughly translates to *'the pleasure that comes from delighting in other people's well-being'*. There is no English word for it. Perhaps there is some merit in combining modern science with ancient wisdom.

Key Takeaways

- Envy is a great equalizer. We all go through it in some shape or form.
- We tend to envy people who are relevant to us and those whose body of work is similar to ours.
- Benign envy is when we want to emulate the object of our envy. It augments performance in many cases.
- Malignant envy is when we wish ill for other people.
- Aim for 'mudita', finding pleasure in the success of others.

CHAPTER 25

NEGOTIATING THE NON-NEGOTIABLE

Identity politics offers an interesting lens to understand presidential twitter wars and self-sabotaging moves which are common these days. Let's analyse the Amazon rainforest fire controversy of the year 2019. Brazilian President Jair Bolsonaro initially said that he would reject the USD 20 million G7 aid package, in effect telling the other nations to mind their own business, only to later lay out terms for the aid's acceptance. He said that he would accept the offer if his French counterpart apologized for criticizing his handling of the fires and granted him exclusive rights to disburse the aid money.

Simply put, identity politics is the process of positioning our identity to get what we want. It unfolds at all levels of daily life and influences resources we have access to. Unless we are attuned to the power of identity politics, we will become its unwitting pawn. These are four strategies that can help us navigate the trap of identity politics. While they are designed for the workplace, most of them also hold true for tricky personal situations.

First, map the political landscape. Key decision makers are contextual. Depending upon the situation at hand, we need to identify who they are, what they care about and create synergies between their priorities and ours. In most cases, we cannot do this alone. We need the support of our informal support structure, especially people who are also trusted by the key decision makers. This is critical in case we don't see eye to eye with the key decision makers or if they don't trust us.

Second, be aware of intentional and unintentional blockers. There are always people who are keen on sabotaging agreements because their identity feels threatened by new relationships and reconciliations. They go out of the way, often secretly, to botch negotiations. As a thought experiment, let's take a leader of a G7 country who profits out of the confrontation between Brazil and France. He would do whatever it takes to bring the negotiation to a halt while on the surface appearing to be a strong proponent of rapprochement. While in most cases blockers don't become strong allies, we can mitigate the damage by partially adapting our stance to accommodate their fears.

Third, design an inclusive decision-making process. Despite our efforts to foster collaboration, sometimes people can feel excluded and work behind the scenes to sabotage things. That's where Harvard International Negotiation Program founder Daniel Shapiro's ECNI (Exclude, Consult, Negotiate, Inform) method provides a useful framework. It states that different stakeholders influence decision-making differently. We need to exclude block-ers, consult with mentors, negotiate with key decision makers or their trusted allies and inform everyone involved. Using the ECNI method, we can streamline decisions and make the process more inclusive.

Fourth, be generous. No matter how hard we try, people can and will use identity politics against us. That is why it is important to take pre-emptive action. The most effective strategy is to be gener-ous and put conscious effort in being less threatening. Generosity is the most potent and resilient source of power. It expands influence, enhances structural power and increases trust.

While generosity increases overall trust, it doesn't automatically make us less threatening. We need to be seen as an ally chasing a shared goal. Being perceived as a threat has absolutely no advantage. Even if people admire you, they will do whatever they can to ensure you don't get what you want. Simply put, we need to persistently position ourselves as people who maximize partnerships and minimize resentment.

Next time you are in a high stress environment at work or involved with multiple teams, try and identify the strands of identity politics. Wherever there are people, there is politics. I hope this four-pronged strategy will be a useful tool in your arsenal to deal with such situations.

Key Takeaways
- Identity politics is the process of positioning our identity to get what we want.
- Map out the key decision makers.
- Keep the blockers in mind.
- Make decision-making inclusive.
- Be generous. It can be your superpower.

CHAPTER 26

WHY WAGE TRANSPARENCY MATTERS

Network Capital has an anonymous posting feature where millennials seek advice from community members without disclosing their identity. Usually, such posts are about exploring jobs and pursuing higher studies. Since the risk of being identified by their managers and colleagues is mitigated, people tend to be more forthright.

Last week, we got a message from a senior product manager with a distinguished academic and professional record. She spoke multiple languages, built great products and consistently exceeded expectations. She had noteworthy patents in electrical engineering and her humanitarian work had been recognized by the United Nations. In the year 2016, she joined one of the largest fintech companies and ranked among the top 5 per cent performers for three years straight.

Things were going great until she accidently learned that the newly hired associate she was supposed to mentor, would be joining at the same stock level and making more money from day one, than her current salary. This baffled her as they graduated from the same engineering school and worked under the same professor. She had much more work experience, more patents, better grades and strong performance indicators on the job. The only apparent difference was gender and colour.

Her instinctive reaction was to write a scathing mail to her manager. Thankfully, she remembered Abraham Lincoln's 'hot letter', a practice famous for turning rivals into allies. Lincoln would pile all his anger in a note and put it aside until his emotions cooled down. That's exactly what our community member did. She drafted an angry email but didn't send it.

We have several interesting data points and mental models to draw upon: Gender pay gap has been studied extensively and we have enough empirical evidence to account for its existence.

In most developed countries, women are paid less than men for the same work. According to the statistical office of the European Union (EU), for every USD 100 earned by a man, a woman earns USD 78.50 in Germany, USD 79 in the United Kingdom and USD 83.80 on average across EU countries. In every OECD (Organisation for Economic Co-operation and Development) member country, men are paid more than women. Averaging 13.5 per cent, the gap ranges from 36.7 per cent in South Korea to 3.4 per cent in Luxembourg. This gap persists, despite the universal attention it has received, and it is even 'widening' in some cases.

One solution is wage transparency. In Sweden, you can find out anyone's salary with a simple phone call. Businesses with 25 or more employees have to establish an equality action plan. And companies with big pay gaps face fines if they do not establish it. In simple words, the Swedes have made it easier to talk about wage inequity. Naysayers might suggest that examples from Nordic countries aren't representative. Let's explore if that's the case.

In the year 2015, PayScale surveyed more than 70,000 American employees. The study demonstrated that the more people knew about why they earn what they earn, especially in relation to their peers, the less likely they were to quit. Dave Smith, Chief Product and Strategy Officer at PayScale said, 'Open and honest discussion around pay was found to be more important than typical measures of employee engagement.'

A Professor at INSEAD, Morten Bennedsen, collaborated with Columbia Business School and Cornell University researchers to conduct an empirical study to demonstrate the impact of mandatory wage transparency. It turns out that in almost every context, disclosing gender disparities in pay narrows the wage gap. Further, employees are more motivated when salaries are transparent. They work harder, are more productive and collaborate more with colleagues. Wage transparency isn't a panacea, but evidence clearly suggests that it is worth a try.

No matter how compelling the case for wage transparency, we can't ask our community member to wait for it to become standard practice. She needs to act now. What should she do?

The first step is to congratulate herself for not sending that angry email. That unsent angry email will ultimately get her the much deserved raise and promotion. With a clear mind, she should write down her negotiation goal and talk to peers in other fintech companies, something she should have done when she took this job.

Tech companies tend to be very intuitive about such issues and are competitive about top talent. With her track record, she is likely to get competing offers from other companies in no time. This will serve as the basis for her counter-negotiation.

With the offer in hand, she should have an honest conversation with her manager where she makes her case and explains how this episode made her feel. If her manager offers a reasonable explanation and a tangible career development plan, she should consider staying.

Of course, bringing her salary equal to the new hire is unacceptable. Why? Her company never wanted her to find out that she was being underpaid. It is time for them to take corrective action otherwise their colourful diversity poster will be nothing more than a sham.

Key Takeaways

- Never send an angry email.
- Disclosing gender disparities in pay narrows the wage gap.
- Wage transparency deserves to be tried out. Evidence supports it.
- Negotiate when you have leverage.

CHAPTER 27

HOW FRUSTRATION LEADS TO INNOVATION

Thomas Edison didn't invent light bulbs, he improved key design features. Tristan Walker didn't invent razors, he customized them for African–American men. Dyson didn't invent vacuum cleaners, he fixed a major engineering flaw. Even though none of them invented products they are best known for, their genius was to channelize their individual frustrations into practical innovations. Start-ups, governments and corporations devote copious amounts of time, resources and brainpower to try and foster innovation. Unfortunately, not much comes out of it.

Scott Chacon, co-founder and former Chief Information Officer (CIO) of GitHub suggests that the most effective way to be innovative is to find your frustration and figure out how best to fix it. Being a champion of first-principle thinking, Chacon suggests we get to the root of our frustration and ask what should it be like in an ideal world and what we need to do to get there.

Most of the great innovations emerge from reimagining things we have either accepted or taken for granted. A major difference between great innovators and the rest of us is that we let our frustration pile on and expect others to solve it. Another differentiating factor is grit or the ability to persevere despite obstacles.

James Dyson spent years tinkering in his backyard till he came up with the dual cyclone bagless vacuum cleaner. This was in the pre-internet era, so he had to manually conduct thousands of design experiments. Even the tiniest of flaws meant that he had to rerun the entire experiment from scratch. Instead of getting tired, he accelerated his pace of tinkering by making copious notes about what worked and what didn't.

Today, Dyson Ltd is a multi-billion-dollar company. Similarly, Tristan Walker, despite his pedigreed education and work experience, was rejected by almost every VC. Instead of giving up, he strengthened his resolve to create a product that truly addressed the grooming needs of African–American men. Today, his company is among the largest subscription businesses in the world.

British music producer, Brian Eno who has collaborated with the likes of David Bowie, U2, Coldplay, innately understands the value of creativity boosts induced by frustration. He partnered with artist Peter Smith to produce the *Oblique Strategies*, a deck of cards designed to break artists out of creative blocks with the use of frustrating constraints. Legend has it that once drummer Phil Collins got so frustrated with Eno's unpredictable requests that he started throwing beer cans around the studio. The final album was a masterpiece, but Collins resented it at the time.

Through the Network Capital accessibility subgroup, I learned how the frustration of dealing with infrastructural challenges led to innumerable innovations for and by people with physical disabilities.

Nipun, one of our community members, cannot lift his hands against gravity and hence cannot pick up a glass or a cup. With the help of his mother, he learned how to have everything with a straw. When it came to eating, he would turn another bowl upside down so that he would get a raised platform to balance his hand. More than convenience, these innovations made him independent. He could finally decide when and how much to drink and eat.

Nipun travels extensively for work and has often grappled with the frustration of not getting access to physically-disabled friendly toilets. A few years ago, after checking into a hotel near Lucknow, he learned that the toilet door was too narrow for his wheelchair. He had no choice but to work with his attendant and remove the door thereby creating the two extra inches for his wheelchair to enter.

Many path-breaking innovations are a direct result of frustrations faced by persons with disabilities. The first variant of text messaging used Teletype machines with 5-bit Baudot code which was actually invented for the deaf. Another interesting story is of Alexander Graham Bell. He first became interested in sound because his mother was deaf. The frustration of not being able to communicate with her gave him the motivation to eventually invent the telephone.

Some of our best ideas emerge from grappling with frustration but we do our best to wipe it out of our lives. What if we embraced it? What if we occasionally introduced mess in our lives? What if we let our frustrations propel our innovations? Perhaps being frustrated will be less frustrating and more rewarding.

Key Takeaways

- Innovation is often a result of fixing our most frustrating challenges.
- Difference between innovators and the rest of us is that we let our frustration build and expect others to solve it.
- Negotiating with frustration is inconvenient but worth it.

CHAPTER 28

MILLENNIALS HAVE A SUBSCRIPTION POWERED FUTURE

American Rapper Kanye West is popularly called the first SaaS (software-as-a-service) musician. In the year 2016, he launched *The Life of Pablo,* an unfinished album where he kept tweaking the lyrics based on feedback from his fans and constantly changed the order of songs. Using techspeak, he launched an MVP (minimal viable product) and reimagined his customers into subscribers and creative participants.

In the digital age, we prefer outcomes to ownership and customization to standardization. That is why subscription is the future of business and every company is doing its best to become a subscription company as soon as possible. This trend goes beyond business.

WHY SUBSCRIPTION WORKS

Companies that run on subscription models grow their revenue more than nine times faster than S&P500, stock performance of 500 largest companies. There are three reasons why subscriptions work for businesses in the digital age.

First, they expand optionality for the customer. If customers aren't satisfied, switching to another service provider is straight forward.

Second, subscriptions transform transactions into meaningful relationships. Instead of focusing on one-time sale, entrepreneurs need to provide value over an extended period of time. This is a win-win scenario. Entrepreneurs work hard to understand unmet customer needs and figure out innovative means to provide services that go beyond the expectations of the underlying contract. This makes the service provider better and enhances customer surplus.

Lastly, subscriptions ease out the financial burden of customers. Instead of committing a sizable chunk of their savings to acquiring assets, they can avail the desired services for a fraction of the cost. Let's see this in action. Cars are depreciating assets. The moment we drive them out of the showroom, their value drops by almost 50 per cent. That is why subscription services like Porche Passport appeals to millennials. They can drive the latest Porsche car models for as long as they want without having to deal with the headaches of ownership. All this at a cost that is both affordable and attractive.

BUILDING A SUBSCRIPTION CULTURE

Every MBA student learns about the four 'P's in Marketing 101: product, price, promotion and place. Today, product ownership is dead. Hence the first of four 'P's is better understood as service. With that in mind, we can repivot the entire business to focus on customer satisfaction.

Tien Tzuo (CEO, Zuora) offers a great framework to visualize any company as an integrated organization of subsystems tied to what the customer truly wants. He suggests that organizations need to incentivize radical collaboration across organizational silos and constantly evolve to delight customers. This might be chaotic in the short term, but it brings organizations closer to what they intend to achieve.

Today, the whole world runs as a service: education, transportation, media, healthcare and even government. While subscriptions are not entirely a new idea, ubiquitous internet connectivity coupled with decreasing infrastructure cost and high levels of customer awareness have made subscriptions the perfect complements to businesses in the digital age.

In the year 2002, commenting on the decline of iTunes-style downloads, Steve Jobs said that the subscription model was bankrupt and destined to fail. The same year song-writer and actor David Bowie made a far more prescient statement: 'Music subscriptions are going to become like running water of electricity.'

While Jobs got most things right, he underestimated the power of subscriptions—the heart and soul of businesses in the digital age. Perhaps Bowie saw what Jobs couldn't.

Key Takeaways
- We prefer outcomes to ownership.
- Today, the world runs as a service.
- Subscriptions transform transactions to relationships.
- Subscriptions have already changed the nature of business and the future of jobs.

CHAPTER 29

WHAT YOU DO IS WHO YOU ARE

A lesser known fact about serial entrepreneur and VC, Ben Horowitz, is that he failed to build a career as a hip-hop artist. Even though he couldn't do much in music, the training came in handy later in his career. In fact, his new book *What You Do Is Who You Are* draws upon many references from hip hop to explain how strong cultures are built and how they apply to modern workplaces.

As an entrepreneur, setting the culture of your organization can be exceptionally hard and there is a stark shortage of reliable reference material. Most management books suffer from survivorship bias. They tend to focus on companies that succeeded and incorrectly conclude that their culture made them thrive.

The beauty of Horowitz's book is that it doesn't reverse engineer. He offers five guiding principles of building a culture that enables great work.

First, virtues are far more important than values. The reason why efforts to establish corporate values are basically worthless is that they emphasize beliefs instead of actions. Unfortunately, there is a huge difference between what companies claim to stand for and how its employees behave. Culture isn't colourful walls and sushi lunches. It is composed of daily micro-behaviours. You can claim to champion whatever you want but your actions reveal your true self.

Here it is important to keep in mind that role modelling helps but doesn't work when companies scale.

When Horowitz was the CEO of Loudcloud, he assumed that if he led by example, other employees will follow suit. However, as the company grew and diversified, its culture became a random aggregation of subcultures fostered under different managers.

Second, accelerate the contradictions. Horowitz redefines Karl Marx's quote to explain that how the hypocrisy and contradictions in companies can turn out to be great learning opportunities if management teams try to understand their origin. Specifically, teams need to identify what actions widen the chasm between espoused values and virtues. Horowitz openly says that without this principle, Loudcloud would never have achieved the success it did.

Third, culture doesn't eat strategy for breakfast. There has been a false dichotomy between culture and strategy for a long time. Today, if entrepreneurs and founders wish to build a business that lasts and accomplishes something meaningful, they need to ensure that both culture and strategy reinforce each other.

That is why I am a big proponent of diversity champions being part of the core team formulating the overall strategy. Having a leader of diversity doesn't work if she doesn't have a seat at the strategy table.

Fourth, shocking rules reinforce cultural priorities at the time. In the early days of Facebook, 'Move fast and break things' was the acceptable operating principle. Obviously, Mark Zuckerberg wasn't telling his engineers to be reckless without reason. He knew that in order to succeed in a network-led business and overcome competition from incumbents like MySpace, he had to prioritize speed over everything else. Moving fast was the need of the hour and the shocking by-product of breaking things was the acceptable side effect. Precisely because it was shocking that engineers understood the trade-off.

In 2014, Facebook's shocking rule made way for the much more stable motto: 'Move fast with stable infrastructure.' It was less shocking but indicated the priority of the organization at the time—risk mitigation. As Horowitz explains, cultures evolve with mission and stage of implementation.

Fifth, make ethics explicit. The most common mistake founders make is that they assume employees will do the right thing even when it conflicts with other objectives and incentives. If you want to observe ethics in your organization, observe the behaviour of sales people on the last day of the quarter. Their actions will demonstrate the culture and ethical index of your organization.

Contrary to popular belief, being ethical isn't a liability. It can strengthen your culture and be a huge competitive advantage. Toussaint Louverture, the leader of the slave revolt in Haiti, used ethics as a way to elevate culture, and build trust at one of the harshest periods in history. Ultimately, it created an army that was much more principled than its adversaries and overcame the British, French and Spanish forces despite being severely under-resourced.

By presenting examples like Louverture and offering insightful culture design principles from hip hop art, Horowitz does what most others have failed to do—demystify culture. The single biggest takeaway for me was that culture is not preordained. It is very much a function of our actions. What we do is truly who we are.

Key Takeaways

- Virtues are more important than values.
- Get to the bottom of contradictions.
- Culture and strategy need to reinforce each other.
- Shocking rules reinforce core priorities.
- Being ethical is profitable in the long term.

CHAPTER 30

GROUPS THAT SING TOGETHER STAY TOGETHER

Last year, I witnessed Vienna Boys' Choir mesmerize Delhi with renditions of western classical, Indian and indie-fusion music. These 22 boys aged between 9 and 14 years came from 15 countries and even included a Syrian refugee who augmented the conductor's piano with his *Oud*, a pear shaped Middle-Eastern musical instrument. I was struck not only by their team-work but also by how they united all of us sitting in Kamani Auditorium. They engaged us effortlessly and it felt like we were creating the music together.

Dr Eiluned Pearce, a postdoctoral research associate in experimental psychology at the University of Oxford, has explored why singing creates such a sense of solidarity. Upon analysing educational charities and musical ensembles in United Kingdom, she and her team came to the conclusion that singing bonds newly formed groups much faster than other communal activities.

The larger lessons from her work could help start-ups, corporates and even non-profits who spend disproportionate resources trying to build a sense of community among employees. Think of all the offsites, motivational posters, colourful walls and inspiring speakers—they are designed to increase the sense of solidarity among working groups. Unfortunately, most of these interventions fail to deliver.

In one of my first jobs after college, the HR official proudly walked the new employees through a long, sleep-inducing presentation of interest-based subgroups in the organization. It was filled with pictures of employees playing cricket, dancing, cooking and painting. Reluctantly, I joined the subgroups and waited for the next steps. The wait turned out to be longer than I had anticipated. By the time I left the organization, I got just two notifications from my subgroups—one about the fact that there had been no activity for a long time and the other that the subgroup was being deactivated.

Such is the fate of most interest-based subgroups and communities within organizations. So, should we take a leaf out of Dr Pearce's research and have all employees sing together? The answer is obviously no. Forcing a reluctant singer to join a band or a choir for strengthening organizational culture could seriously backfire.

However, we could use the same principles that make singing together meaningful to design opportunities for inter-personal bonding within organizations. Dr Pearce collaborated with Workers' Educational Association, a British non-profit organization, to test if singing is the only way to enhance bonding. It turns out that other interest-based activities such as creative writing and crafts have very similar effects. The only difference is that they tend to be a bit slower than singing.

In order to apply Dr Pearce's research into practice, organizations should consider a three-pronged approach. First, they need to be intentional about design principles of employee engagement. A one-off event or an offsite or a talk by a celebrity doesn't work. Interesting group activities need to have the same cadence as conference calls.

The Vienna Boys' Choir is something students participate in over and above their academic commitments at school. They enjoy practicing regularly and strengthen bonds with fellow choristers through the process. What if organizations encouraged and supported such intra-company, communal passion projects?

Second, they need to be inclusive. The HR officials or your managers should not be the only ones deciding how and who you bond with in office. Beyond administrative activities, day-to-day management and coaching, they are better off following the light-touch model of college festivals where students from different departments organically come together to organize events on a shoestring budget.

Imagine this in office! Employees from different teams coming together do participate in activities they truly care about. A natural by-product of this engagement would be cross-functional knowledge exchange.

Lastly, companies need to stop measuring cosmetic metrics. As rocket scientist turned law professor Ozan Varol says, 'We track what's easy to track—not what's important—and falsely assume that if we hit these metrics, we accomplished something valuable.' Every company is unique in the way it operates. The ways employees bond with each other at NASA could be very different from their peers at Nike. That is why it is important to pick contextually relevant metrics that are closely aligned with both business objectives and personal preferences of employees.

Moments before Vienna Boys' Choir left the stage, I noticed a twinkle in the eyes of the conductor. The boys had made him proud, and in that moment, I swear we were all infinite.

Key Takeaways

- Singing bonds newly formed groups much faster than other communal activities.
- The same principles that make singing an effective bonding experience can be used to strengthen organizational cultures.
- To make it happen, companies need to be intentional about design principles, be inclusive and stop measuring cosmetic metrics.

CHAPTER 31

THE AVENGERS AND DIVERSITY QUOTIENT

I loved watching *Avengers: Endgame*. It was phenomenal not only because of its gripping plot but also because it took me back to business school when we watched *12 Angry Men* to learn more about nuances of negotiations. I think *Avengers: Endgame* should be taught as a case study in all graduate programmes. In addition to being wickedly interesting, it is sprinkled with insights on leadership, strategy and organizational behaviour.

What fascinated me most was the way the Avengers came together to pursue an almost impossible challenge, a moonshot in tech-speak. Each team member had a clear sense of purpose, shared understanding of the goal, acute awareness of potential challenges and most importantly, skin in the game. Many qualified teams in start-ups and corporates fail because networking dinners and offsites cannot be substitutes for a unifying mission.

Best-selling author, Simon Sinek's book, *Start with Why*, explains that unless we agree on the why, the what and the how are meaningless. This concept is especially important when we are putting together a team for a moonshot project. We mustn't settle for hiring smart people who can do the job. It is far better to hire motivated people who believe what we believe and are willing to learn, sacrifice and bring new dimensions to the mission.

It is worth noting that sharing a belief system doesn't mean hiring people like you. If the Avengers did that, the villain Thanos would have had a blissful retirement in Planet 0259-S, referenced as the garden in the movie.

It is well known that diversity of gender, thought, conviction and action, enables better problem-solving. One often ignored category is cognitive diversity which is essentially the difference in perspective or information processing styles. Tackling new challenges requires striking a balance between what we know and learning what we don't know at an accelerated pace. According to two United Kingdom based professors, Alison Reynolds and David Lewis, high degree of cognitive diversity generates accelerated learning and performance in the face of new, uncertain and complex situations. Cognitive diversity and complementarity of skills were probably the two most crucial factors that powered the Avengers to a well-deserved victory.

If cognitive diversity is so crucial, why don't modern workplaces encourage them? The truth is that many start-ups and corporates try but often stumble into two bottlenecks. First, cognitive diversity is hard to detect from the outside. Reynolds and Lewis state that it cannot be predicted or easily orchestrated. Being from a different culture or generation gives insufficient clues as to how a person processes information and responds to change. The second reason is that there are cultural barriers to cognitive diversity. People prefer to fit into the organizational culture than to question the way things get done.

One of the biggest mistakes organizations make is to only hire people who fit into their existing culture. They should instead hire for cultural contribution. In practical terms this means empowering employees to evolve and shape cultural norms.

Another vital lesson from *Avengers: Endgame* was the art of influencing and motivation. How the characters Captain America, Black Widow and Ant-Man convinced Iron Man to join the team was a useful lesson in getting a reluctant person to say yes. Even the intimate discussion between Iron Man and Pepper Potts offers a beautiful spectacle into how functional couples take challenging professional decisions. The key insight to getting a 'yes' in such situations is understanding how your team member or partner operates, lay out what is at stake, paint the vision for future and help them arrive at the decision. If you push too hard at the wrong time, you might spook them.

Key Takeaways

- Cognitive diversity is a critical tool for effective problem-solving.
- Cognitive diversity is hard to detect from the outside.
- There are cultural barriers to enabling cognitive diversity.
- Hire for cultural contribution, not cultural fit.

CHAPTER 32

WHAT START-UPS CAN LEARN FROM FLEA MARKETS

Spread over 17 million square feet, the Dubai Global Village is perhaps the world's largest tourism and entertainment project. The entire space is designed like a flea market and combines cultures of 90 countries. During the three hours I walked around the Global Village, local manufacturers and artisans tried to sell me everything under the sun—from Yemeni honey and Egyptian perfumes to Bosnian kebabs and Irani rugs.

I was amazed by their negotiation skills and sales techniques. Without any business training, these artisans had mastered story-telling and learned the art of connecting with customers of different age groups, cultures and nationalities. The more time I spent in the Global Village, the more I realized that start-ups can learn important lessons from flea markets.

The first thought that crossed my mind was finding talent. I wondered, 'What if these artisans were to sell software products instead of soaps and oils? What if start-ups were to hire them as frontline salespeople or customer success managers?'

Unlike marketing, finance or strategy, sales is not taught in most business schools. The underlying belief is that one can't learn to sell by reading books and attending lectures. If one doesn't learn selling in classrooms, getting hands-on practice is the only way forward. That is why these local artisans are likely to turn out to be champion salespeople. What they lack in academic qualifications and industry-specific experience, they make up with an intimate understanding of business.

Hiring these artisans not only makes practical sense but also adds to the diversity quotient of the modern workplace. It is time for start-ups and mature businesses to go beyond their myopic definitions of diversity. Instead of going to the same schools and looking for candidates with big brands on their CVs, it is worth considering an entirely unexplored talent pool.

My second takeaway was cost efficiency. The entire Global Village is divided into conclaves representing different countries. Within each conclave, there are dozens of shops run by local artisans. They manage their inventory, operate account books, run offline campaigns and also pay rent—all this on a shoestring budget. There is no external capital—venture or otherwise—so the only way to survive is to keep a tab on revenues and costs. Such operational efficiency is a valuable lesson for start-ups that liberally spend on marketing and customer acquisition without figuring out a business model.

The third thing that struck me was how well these artisans knew their customers. Even though most customers were walking into the Global Village for the first time, years of dealing with similar groups had given them a strong sense of the tastes and preferences of their customers. Based on the speed of walking, group size, gender mix and sartorial choice, they would decide what to pitch and how.

After being convinced to try hundreds of Middle-Eastern perfumes in different shopping booths, I learned how the artisans had mastered the magician's choice, a verbal technique employed by magicians to nudge the audience towards an outcome. I am not saying that these artisans are the only ones using such techniques, but they are the ones making it work with effortless charm.

Many start-ups rely entirely on data to know their customers. While the data-driven approach is commendable, it must be complemented by actual engagement with customers. Data coupled with ethnographic insights from customer engagement can help start-ups truly understand the tastes and preferences of their customers.

My final takeaway came from the Yemeni booth. That's where I learned how the artisans balanced competition with collaboration. Honey from Yemen is among the best in the world. I stopped to try out flavours at different stalls. Each stall was competing hard for every customer and it was hard to tell one apart from the other. I stopped at the first stall I saw and was about to purchase. That's when I discovered that the only bottles this stall had were 500 ml ones, about five times the size allowed in check-in luggage. I explained my predicament to the stall manager and without any hesitation, he pointed me to his competitor who had smaller cases and travel-friendly pouches.

Instead of obsessing over undercutting competitors, start-ups should be driven by solving customers' problems. As long as competition and collaboration are driven by serving the customer, it makes entrepreneurial sense. More importantly, it is the right thing to do.

Growing up, my brother and I would accompany our parents to neighbourhood flea markets in Delhi. It would be a family picnic of sorts. Now we live in different parts of the world and the flea marker adventure has made way for the efficiency of e-commerce platforms. Going to the Global Village Dubai brought back fond memories and also gave me precious business lessons to think about.

Key Takeaways

- Skills are transferable. Keep an eye out on people doing a great job in any sector.
- Cost efficiency drives innovation.
- One can both compete and collaborate.

CHAPTER 33

WHY THE MODERN WORKPLACE NEEDS MORE REBELS

'Osteria Francescana' is a three Michelin star restaurant run by a rebel Italian chef Massimo Bottura. It was rated as the best restaurant in the world in the year 2016 and its charm lies in the way it flips tradition on its head. One of the most famous dishes at Bottura's restaurant is 'Oops I dropped the lemon tart'. Its origin is quite literal. One evening the chef responsible for desserts accidentally dropped a lemon tart. Instead of screaming at him, Bottura invented a new dessert—a smashed lemon tart served on a colourful plate—which has since then emerged as the most popular order at the restaurant.

Bottura is what Professor Francesca Gino, author of *Rebel Talent: Why It Pays to Break the Rules at Work and in Life* calls a positive deviance rebel. During her research that analysed people who cheat and behave dishonestly in organizations, she stumbled across innumerable stories of people who broke rules in a way that created a net positive change in their organizations and in the world. Unlike the cheats, such rebels tend to share five talents: novelty, curiosity, perspective, diversity and authenticity.

Unfortunately, despite all the talk about diversity and innovation, most organizations make rebels feel unwelcome. According to a recent survey conducted across a wide range of sectors, industries and seniority levels, nearly 50 per cent of the respondents said that they regularly feel the pressure to conform. This leads to decreased engagement, dwindled productivity and suffocating work environment.

The good news is that constructive rebelliousness can be augmented both at a personal and organizational level. Leveraging Professor Gino's eight-pronged framework of rebel leadership, organizations can transform the disengaged rebels into engaged contributors. These points are equally relevant for freelancers and solopreneurs.

First, seek out the new. It is important to add an element of surprise, disrupt monotonous routines and seek inspiration from different fields. Rebels thrive in unfamiliar contexts as the joy of discovery creates a sense of adventure at work. Richard Feynman came up with his Nobel Prize winning physics insight by watching someone play with plates and dishes at Cornell University's cafeteria. Novelty inspires innovation.

Second, encourage constructive dissent. We tend to surround ourselves with people like ourselves. Rebels, on the other hand, thrive in healthy conflict and learn from those who don't share their worldview. Instead of incentivizing confirmation and consensus, leaders should reward contrarian insights.

Third, open conversations, don't close them. Both rebels and improv comedians have one thing in common: They use the phrase 'yes, and...' constructively. This allows them to learn from and add value to a wide spectrum of conversations. Given that innovative ideas tend to emerge from combining different strands of thoughts, it is no small wonder that rebels are the epicentre of disruption.

Fourth, reveal yourself and reflect. Trust builds when we share our imperfect selves and reflect on how to serve our stakeholders better. Rebels tend to practice radical candour which might be uncomfortable for some in the short term but eventually benefits everyone.

Fifth, learn everything—then forget everything. Constructive rebels master fundamentals but never become slaves to the rules. Rather than disrespecting traditions and breaking rules simply for the sake of it, effective rebels develop a deep understanding of the basic concepts. Before reinventing beloved Italian recipes, Massimo Bottura spent months studying them and understanding the rationale behind each step.

Sixth, find freedom in constraints. Some of the most creative pieces of literature were written by authors while they had day jobs. Harper Lee was an airline ticketing agent; Franz Kafka was an insurance clerk; and Agatha Christie used to be an assistant pharmacist. Each of them transformed their time constraints into creativity and focus.

Seventh, lead from the trenches. Rebels enjoy having skin in the game and taking up challenging tasks. They tend to be driven by impact more than procedures.

Lastly, foster happy accidents. Chef Bottura creates happy accidents by hiring people from different countries to give traditional dishes an unconventional flavour. Steve Jobs achieved the same goal by designing the headquarters of Pixar Animation Studios to have a massive open atrium where people who do not usually work together would bump into one another and strike up conversations.

This framework is not only for those who identify as rebels. Being a rebel isn't binary; all of us fall on a spectrum. It boils down to bringing our true selves to work and feeling free to express unpopular opinions. The modern workplace should create conditions to tap the inner rebel of employees not only because it strengthens organizational culture but also because it adds unique business and social value.

Key Takeaways

- Rebels are easy to talk about but difficult to embrace. More than 50 per cent employees feel pressure to conform.
- Rebels share five talents: novelty, curiosity, perspective, diversity and authenticity.
- Everyone is a rebel to some extent. Some of us embrace it and some let it go.
- Rebels strengthen organizational culture and add business value.
- To unleash your inner rebel and make it work for you, follow the eight principles of rebel leadership.

CHAPTER 34

LET'S STOP TALKING ABOUT GENERATION GAPS

Paul Tassner is one of Network Capital's oldest members. He was fired at the age of 64. On a sunny Friday evening, just before Christmas, he was called into a meeting that turned out to be his exit interview. His wife had no idea about it and was waiting for him at a nearby restaurant. A few hours later, they both got drunk and celebrated the end of 40 years of continual employment.

He could have retired but chose a different path. Combining his engineering skills and passion for environment, Paul started making biodegradable packaging from waste and became a first-time entrepreneur at the age of 66. Over the past few years, his company has won dozens of innovation awards and seen a significant spike in revenues. Paul's TED Talk has been viewed more than two million times and he is on a mission to make the phrase '70 over 70' as common as '30 under 30'.

Entrepreneurship and creativity should be age-blind, he says. I asked Paul if he had any advice for today's millennials. In his inimitable style, he said that perhaps they should try and learn more from older colleagues.

Chip Conley was 52 years old when he got a call from the founders of Airbnb to help them guide their growth from a high growth start-up to a mature company. By that time, he hadn't heard of the sharing economy, didn't have Uber or Lyft on his phone and had no idea what shipping a product meant. His past experience of building boutique hotels was relevant, but it would be useless if the engineering team didn't trust him. Instead of judging them or doubting himself, he set upon the task of building a shared language for the entire organization. Together they figured out a way to make multi-generational wisdom work, charted a common set of goals and pursued them relentlessly. Under Chip's mentorship, from the year 2013 to 2017, Airbnb's valuation increased by a multiple of 12 and it even managed to become profitable.

Leaders like Chip and Paul have proven that sharing economy is as much about sharing wisdom across generations as it is about sharing resources. That's why the concept of mutual mentorship across generations strongly resonates with me. I set up Network Capital with the belief that everyone has something to learn and something to teach. All we need is a platform and a community to share skills at scale across barriers, borders, generations and boundaries.

This is, of course, easier said than done. We have a natural tendency to gravitate towards people we relate to, those with whom we have a lot in common. They tend to be similar in age, conviction, taste and outlook. That is why marketing gurus and political pundits lay so much faith in customer and voter segmentation.

The term generation gap traces its origin to sociologist Karl Mannheim's *Theory of Generations* but it only became mainstream in the 1960s when the younger generation (now called baby boomers) seemed to go against everything their parents stood for in terms of music, politics, career choices and government views.

I feel that in the coming years, as people live longer, retire later and change jobs more frequently, we will witness up to five generations work on the same team or in the same office. Today, almost 40 per cent of Americans have bosses younger than them.

This trend is likely to replicate itself in other countries. Instead of swallowing this as a bitter pill, we can go the Airbnb route and make generational diversity work for us.

Chip famously said that companies are not B-to-B (business to business) or B-to-C (business-to-consumer). They are H-to-H (human-to-human). With the mainstreaming of AI, building scalable H2H businesses will need wisdom across generations. That's why it is time to stop talking about generation gap and start exploring inter-generational synergy.

Key Takeaways

- In the coming years, five generations would be working on the same team/in the same office.
- People will have to learn to reinvent themselves multiple times.
- Exploring inter-generational synergies will drive innovation and build a culture of sharing.
- Businesses are driven by human relations and will need inter-generational wisdom.

CHAPTER 35

THE ART OF MAKING A COMPELLING ARGUMENT

In January 2020, I participated in an unusual debate at Raisina Dialogue, a multilateral conference held annually in Delhi. All participants were pre-assigned to different teams and didn't get to choose their stand. As luck would have it, my team had to argue against something we believed in. Although it was quite unsettling to begin with, preparing for the debate strengthened our collective understanding of the subject. It got me thinking if debating can be a tool for learning.

We live in a time when high pitched shouting matches and social media wars are the norm. We are so sure that we are right that we don't really listen to counter-arguments. We make up our minds and then look for proof.

Berkshire Hathaway's Vice Chairman, Charlie Munger, has an interesting mental model for framing arguments and shaping debates. He says that it is irresponsible to have an opinion on any subject if we can't state the arguments for the other side better than our opponents. This takes both effort and rigorous mental discipline. Munger calls it the cost of having an informed opinion.

We have to learn to overcome confirmation bias—favouring information that confirms your previously existing beliefs, train ourselves to see issues through multiple lenses, become our most intelligent critic and have the intellectual honesty to kill some of our most cherished ideas.

Stress-testing our beliefs the way Charlie Munger does empowers us to analyse things from first principles, basic assumptions uncoloured by bias. This strengthens our arguments and enables us to understand weaknesses in our thought process. Most importantly, this iterative approach makes us less dogmatic.

The purpose of having a debate isn't to shove our intellectual superiority over our opponents. It is an opportunity to learn, grow and change our mind when provided with convincing arguments.

Change My View is a Reddit community with almost one million members who have starkly different social, economic and political beliefs. Set up by a Scottish teenager Kal Turnball in the year 2013, it has managed to emerge as a safe digital space for civilized debate. Thousands of people use Kal's platform to change their minds about issues they deeply care about every single day. Recently he partnered with University of Colorado Boulder's Assistant Professor Dr Chenhao Tan and came up with four useful reference points that help explain under what circumstances people change their minds.

First, explaining where you are coming from is far more likely to change someone's mind than well-rehearsed facts and counter-arguments. People care deeply about the rationale underpinning your point of view. Explaining why you hold a particular opinion not only establishes common ground for the conversation but also makes you far more relatable to your opponent.

Second, language plays a subtle yet significant role in the outcome of an argument. Directly quoting someone and finding logical flaws in the statement is usually ineffective. People perceive it as nitpicking their words rather than contradicting their view as a whole.

Additionally, be careful when people use collective words like 'we' in their argument. It is easier to change one person's mind than that of a community. When someone uses 'we', it is often an unconscious way of putting up a barrier against your argument by invoking their affiliation to a larger group. In such cases, you probably won't succeed in changing their mind.

Third, longer replies substantiated by linked references are more effective than short one-liners. Psychologists call backfire effect as the difficulty in accepting that we are wrong. Essentially when our deepest convictions are challenged by contradictory evidence, our beliefs get stronger. Dr Tan's research suggests that we can overcome the backfire effect by addressing different layers of our opponent's arguments and complementing it with trustworthy links.

Fourth, if someone has not changed her mind with three rounds of back and forth arguments, one should agree to disagree. Dr Tan and his team suggest that after the third round, the probability of someone changing their mind drastically reduces.

Of course, these are not foolproof methods but keeping them in mind might help us frame arguments better and inform us which debates are worth engaging in.

As I walked up to the Raisina Dialogue podium to argue something that at least initially I didn't fully believe in, I realized that I not only understood the issue prompt much better but also felt good that I changed my mind. One should have strong opinions that are weakly held. Changing one's mind can be a sign of growth and I am glad that this debate made me realize that.

Key Takeaways

- Debate is an opportunity to learn, not show off.
- Don't make up your mind and then look for proof. Don't be the 'man with a hammer'.
- Explain where you are coming from. Context matters in arguments.
- Language is critical. Longer, referenced replies are more effective than pithy one-liners.
- It is easier to change the opinion of one person than a group.
- If someone hasn't changed her mind with three rounds of back and forth arguments, agree to disagree.

CHAPTER 36

LOOK OUTSIDE YOUR BUILDING

The year 2020 was the 50th anniversary of *World Economic Forum Annual Meeting* in Davos. While there were many debates and discussions around the challenging state of global affairs, it was energizing to learn how some business leaders were harnessing the power of their organizations to solve complex societal challenges like climate change and technological disruption.

In her book *Think Outside the Building: How Advanced Leaders Can Change the World One Small Innovation at a Time*, Harvard Business School professor, Rosabeth Moss Kanter, explains why the world demands a new kind of 'advanced' business leader who makes conscious attempts to solve problems beyond her company. Dr Kanter advances many arguments out of which three struck a chord with me.

First, as research institutions like Pew and a trust scholar Rachel Botsman explain, there has been a massive degradation of public trust in big institutions. In fact, trust in big businesses is at an all-time low. Their credibility, legitimacy and motives are being questioned and people don't believe they are interested in solving problems that adversely affect communities. If business leaders don't regain the trust of their customers, they will lose significant market value in the years to come.

Second, it helps create a strong talent pool. By the year 2025 millennials will comprise 75 per cent of the global workforce. According to PwC's recent Workforce of the Future survey, 88 per cent of millennials today want to work with purpose driven companies that are ethical and sensitive to the communities they serve. By trying to solve important social and environmental issues, business leaders can attract the brightest young leaders to join their organizations. This will create both economic and social value.

Third is the gift of perspective. Often CEOs get so engrossed focused on performance metrics that their business loses sight of why it exists and what problem it is solving. In addition to missing major market shaping trends, such an inward looking approach reinforces existing biases and creates new ones. It is no wonder that businesses that become irrelevant are often those that try to solve the wrong problems, a direct result of being disconnected with society. Intersectionality created by combining internal expertise, sector-specific knowledge and external perspective gained from addressing social issues strengthens your organization's problem-solving arsenal.

While the points above are addressed to business leaders, they are equally applicable to millennials and young executives at work. Ignoring social challenges in our own backyard or thinking that we will address larger issues once we rise up the professional ladder, is naïve. Habits, mental models and problem solving tools are developed by sustained efforts and relentless experimentation. Millennials who want to lead organizations in the future should consider deepening their connect with social issues. It is not only the right thing to do but also a necessary leadership skill for the 21st century.

In order to get into the habit of looking outside the metaphorical box or building, one has to train to connect with individuals and communities that think differently, ones that don't share our worldview. It is convenient to stick with our clique and stay in our comfort zone, but it comes at the cost of learning. We learn and grow most by engaging with diversity of all kinds.

One of my mentors recently told me that we are an average of five people we share most of our time with. Most millennials spend more time with their colleagues than with their families and friends. That is why it is important to be part of multiple working groups at office and partner with them to do our bit to solve challenges that actually move the needle. We may not be able to resolve all systemic challenges immediately but concerted efforts to address them changes our perspective and arms us with unexplored insights that help us grow personally and professionally. This is over and above the sheer joy of feeling connected with a larger mission, something that transcends our day-to-day work.

Two years ago, at the *World Economic Forum Annual Meeting in Davos*, I had organized a roundtable discussion with fellow Global Shapers and the CEO of a technology company. He concluded our wide ranging conversation paraphrasing author Wayne Dyer—'If you change the way you see the world, you change the world you see.' Perhaps that is the need of the hour for all stakeholders—big and small—to change perspective, build coalitions and see global challenges with a different lens, thereby augmenting both shareholder and stakeholder value.

Key Takeaways

- The world demands a new kind of 'advanced' business leader who makes conscious attempts to solve problems beyond her company.
- Millennials who want to lead organizations in the future should consider deepening their connect with social issues.
- Solving social problems beyond our scope of work is the right thing to do and makes practical business sense.

CHAPTER 37

SHOULD YOU DISCUSS POLITICS AT WORK?

Warren Buffet and Charlie Munger are close friends and business partners who have built Berkshire Hathaway, one of the world's largest public companies. Buffet happens to be a democrat and Munger, a republican. They have never had an argument and even today finish each other's sentences or respond with their signature phrase, 'I have nothing to add to what he said.'

From this example, it might seem that it is easy to disagree politically, be friends and have a functional professional relationship. But we all know that is not the case.

Recently, Charlie Munger was on live television and shared that both political parties in the United States have wings that are full of idiots. Although he didn't explicitly state it, he was alluding to Congresswoman Alexandria Ocasio-Cortez's suggestion that modern monetary theory (MMT), which holds that government doesn't need to balance the budget and that budget surpluses hurt the economy, should be part of the larger discussion. Buffet has already criticized MMT and described it as 'danger zone'.

How is it that two vocal business leaders who have diametrically opposite political views arrive at the same conclusion? It is simple. Buffet is not an average democrat and Munger isn't a stereotypical republican.

As much as we want, our co-workers are unlikely to be like Munger or Buffet so should we discuss politics at work? If yes, how? If not, why not?

To answer these questions, I reached out to Network Capital community members. Sixty-three per cent of the respondents (mostly millennials) said that politics should be discussed at work and a whopping 71 per cent shared that they actively discuss politics during the elections season.

In March 2018, a professor at INSEAD, Professor Craig Smith, authored a seminal article titled *Companies Can't Avoid Politics— and Shouldn't Try To*. He makes a case that the days when companies could hide behind the veneer of neutrality are over and even when they don't make overt political statements, they are conveying their stance.

According to Professor Smith, stakeholders, customers and employees actively look for transparency, consistency, materiality and leadership in modern organizations. They demand and hold companies accountable on these parameters because business institutions don't exist in isolation. They are very much a reflection of society. Perhaps that is why many millennials feel that politics cannot be dissociated from work.

According to LinkedIn's culture report, nine out of ten millennials would consider taking a pay cut to work at politically, socially and environmentally conscious companies—those whose mission and values align with their own.

With ubiquity of social media and a steep spike in the number of hours spent in office, personal and professional lives are becoming more intertwined than ever before. Millennials are spending upwards of 12 hours in office and want to be able to bring their true selves to work. Isn't it fair that they should have the freedom and flexibility to talk about whatever they deem appropriate, including but not limited to politics? It is important to note that freedom and flexibility to talk about politics doesn't mean abandoning reason and indulging in shouting matches like our chatty news anchors.

That's why the real question isn't whether we should talk politics at work or not. It is how we should talk about politics and work with colleagues who choose to express different viewpoints. Instead of legislating them, shouldn't we try and address our own bias about safe topics for discussion?

Not having a political opinion or choosing not to express it isn't an achievement. It is a choice, just like wearing politics on our sleeves. I feel that people should feel free to be as political or apolitical as they please as long as it doesn't negatively affect overall organizational productivity.

In business school, one of my learning group mates was a Chinese investment banker whose views on Tibet left me gasping in disbelief. It was uncomfortable to begin with but instead of letting preconceived notions drive our relationship, we made a genuine effort to understand each other's perspective. By the end of the semester, she stuck to her point of view and I stuck to mine, but we did forge a strong friendship premised on mutual respect.

Working with her added new dimensions to my learning, nego-tiating with initial discomfort strengthened my empathy, and dealing with complexities of diverging opinions enhanced my problem-solving skills. All this happened for two reasons. First, we talked about politics and second, we talked about politics the way politicians don't, but should.

Key Takeaways

- The days when companies could hide behind the veneer of neutrality are over.
- People spend almost half their waking hours in office and should have the freedom to talk about what they want as long as they don't affect their work or the work of others.
- You can forge strong bonds with people who vastly disagree with you politically.

CHAPTER 38

THE ART AND SCIENCE OF GATHERINGS

I began the year 2020 by participating in the Asian Forum on Global Governance (AFGG) along with 48 young diplomats, entrepreneurs, academics and policy makers from 28 countries. The rigorous fellowship programme, conducted under Chatham House rules, included back-to-back group discussions, case studies, policy debates and personal reflections that seamlessly transformed a bunch of strangers with different political and social convictions into an intimate community.

I have always been interested in understanding what distinguishes functional groups and communities that thrive from those that do not. It turns out that the answer lies in how they gather and organize themselves. Conflict resolution expert and author Priya Parker has a three-pronged framework for designing gatherings that augment the interconnectedness of communities.

First, have a clearly articulated goal you want to achieve from the gathering. Most meetings and community gatherings—both formal and informal—confuse category with purpose.

Let us understand this with the help of a few examples from everyday life. Team meeting is a category, taking key decisions is the goal. Unfortunately, most meetings at modern workplaces have very specific formats and structures but no clear goals. Similarly, panel discussion is a category, translating that discussion into something tangible is a goal. I have often observed organizers running helter-skelter to put a panel together without figuring out why the discussion is taking place.

We tend to channel all our energy on getting the logistics right—setup, refreshments, venue, etc.—and end up ignoring the people aspect of the gathering. Taking care of logistical issues is important, but it cannot compensate for lack of purpose.

We mistakenly assume that knowing the type of gathering is enough to shape a collective goal. I can think of innumerable instances where I have attended perfectly planned events and offsites where I just couldn't figure what people were trying to accomplish. Also, I had no idea of what I was supposed to do there apart from showing up.

At AFGG, I noticed that every session, even informal ones, had a structure, a goal and most importantly, an element of surprise. This enabled us to co-create a shared adventure.

Second, cause good controversy. Human connections are as threatened by unhealthy peace as by unhealthy conflict. Unhealthy peace occurs when people are afraid to speak their mind and unhealthy conflict is a euphemism for abuse. Both can wreck communities. Parker suggests that the most effective gatherings learn to cultivate good controversy by creating the conditions for it. Safe conversation topics like weather, food and travel are useful to initiate discussions but in order to augment trust and cohesiveness, we need to learn to discuss things that drive our conviction and curiosity.

While most of us have been taught to avoid discussing religion, money and politics over dinner, research suggests that discussing potentially unsafe topics creates stronger community bonds.

Debating different political, social and economic ideologies of community members strengthened the bond of our AFGG fellowship cohort. Was it easy and fun all the time? Of course not. But we learned to distinguish person from perspective.

Third, create a temporary alternative world with pop-up rules. Think of them as temporary constitutions designed to people together. Parker explains that these rules are powerful because they allow us to temporarily change and harmonize our behaviour. They allow us to connect across cultures and make meaning together without having to be the same.

A pop-up rule at AFGG was inverting one's name tag to provide feedback and ask questions. This little ritual made it slightly easier for the introverts to chime in, and helped us build off of each other's ideas in a fun way.

In addition to Parker's three-pronged framework, I have observed a fourth element that creates memorable gatherings and powerful communities—expression of vulnerability. It turns out that groups that are open to sharing vulnerable moments with each other create safe spaces for difficult discussions.

Fellowships like TED, INK, Ashoka and AFGG typically bring together ambitious young professionals who might also have deep anxieties and insecurities. Instead of single-mindedly focusing on professional goals and achievements, talking about failures or sharing vulnerabilities strengthens the collective resilience of the cohort.

The biggest takeaway from the fellowship was listening to and learning from the experiences of other cohort members. As a collective we decided to take some risks and bare our authentic selves. The outcome could have been very different had AFGG been designed differently.

The essence of hosting any memorable community experience or gathering is to figure out its purpose early on. Doing so enables us to repivot from what to why, thereby making it more about people than the process of bringing them together. Remember this the next time you send or accept any invitation.

Key Takeaways

- Memorable community gatherings and experiences have a clear purpose.
- Knowing the type of gathering is not enough to shape its goal.
- Flowers and candles don't make gatherings memorable. People do.
- Unhealthy peace is as destructive as unhealthy conflict. Cause good controversies.
- Pop-up rules help.

CHAPTER 39

WHY IT IS HARD TO MAKE FRIENDS AT WORK

There is an indie coffee shop right next to my office. Every morning, as I wait for my cold brew, I read the newspaper and go through my email. I sit in a corner, plan my day and enjoy the morning breeze scented with freshly roasted coffee. Just when I am about to leave, I invariably bump into another colleague who frequents the same place. We chat for a bit and head upstairs. I consider her my friend. Similarly, I can point to many other colleagues who have become friends either by working on similar projects or simply walking past empty corridors on long evenings with tight deadlines.

That is why it surprised me that making friends at work was hard for millennials. According to a study commissioned by Milkround, a United Kingdom based job board, 65 per cent of those aged between 25 and 34 years struggle with friendships at work. They conducted in-depth interviews with over 2,000 people and found the situation even more grave for those under 25 years of age. Almost half (48 per cent) of this group admitted to having called in sick at least once to avoid a social scene at work.

While analysing this data, it must be kept in mind that United Kingdom is what anthropologists define as a low-context culture.

People in low-context cultures tend to communicate directly with information rather than emotion, have short-term relationships, follow rules and are generally task-oriented. However, even in high context cultures like India, millennials have reported similar challenges, albeit to a slightly lesser degree.

There are four key reasons for the breakdown of workplace friendships among millennials. First, rising stress levels. Stress is an all-consuming emotion. When we are stressed, we tend to close ourselves to new experiences and create an impenetrable wall around us. Second, long-term employment is a thing of the past. Job-hopping is the norm among millennials. Since we don't stick around, we have replaced building long-term relationships with maintaining transitory politeness. Third, with virtual offices and flexible timings, frequency of face-to-face interactions and shared experiences have reduced. Fourth, a dizzying cocktail of time famine and social media has transformed the geometry of relationships. These days, millennials are constantly connected with friends from school and college on social media. It is far easier to keep in touch with old friends than to build new friends in a work setting where there is too much to do in too little time.

Let's start by recognizing that in today's age, work-life balance is a myth. Work is part of life, not an independent entity. If we want to do meaningful work and have a personal life, striving for work-life harmony is a more realistic goal. It encourages us to ask a simple question: How can we tune the notes of work and life to make them sing together?

The first step is to realize that we can't find the harmony between work and life alone. We need a support system, a sense of belonging and a feeling of community. Isn't that what camaraderie or friendship is all about?

According to American Psychological Association, workplace friendships increase happiness, enhance job satisfaction and lead to better decision-making. When people are friends, they trust each other more. This leads to more information sharing and reduced anxiety over who gets credit.

It is a no brainer that organizations should encourage workplace friendships. However, they must realize that dated methods of enhancing bonding like annual retreats and year-end parties have negligible effect on bonding. Thanks to Paul Ingram's research, now we have scientific proof that people don't mix at mixers. They hang out with those they already know and head back home.

That said, the onus of building workplace friendships cannot be on companies entirely. As Dr Tanya Menon explains in her TED Talk, we need to fight our filters, overcome our biases and connect with those we don't know.

Apart from the intrinsic humanity of reaching out, it is worth noting that a large chunk of new work opportunities can be traced back to these informal, serendipitous friendships. Given the importance of such serendipity, companies should invest in building social hubs—community spaces where employees can partake in shared experiences, get to know each other and in time, emerge as friends.

Ping-pong tables and ice creams are so 1999. With so much chatter around AI and personalization, I am sure good companies will figure out how to create meaningful experiences for their time starved future leaders aching to harmonize work and life.

Key Takeaways

- Sixty-five per cent of those aged between 25 and 34 years struggle with friendships at work.
- There are four key reasons for the breakdown of workplace friendships among millennials: stress, job hopping, declining number of in-person meetings and time famine.
- Work is part of life and not a separate entity.
- To augment friendships at work, organizations need to rethink their design principles.
- Millennials need to make concerted efforts to meet new people.

CHAPTER 40

MODERN LOVE: COUPLES THAT WORK

I reconnected with Gianpiero and Jennifer Petriglieri during my reunion at INSEAD. In addition to being Associate Professors at the same institution, they are married and have children together. Recently, I hosted Dr Jennifer on the Network Capital podcast to discuss her new book *Couples That Work*. Over the last five years, she has studied 100 working couples from across the world and come to a puzzling conclusion: Key to relationship bliss for dual-career couples is a psychological contract of sorts.

Simply put, the relationship or psychological contract is a description of the kind of life a couple wants to build together. It isn't binding or prescriptive, but tends to give the relationship a solid foundation. Specifically, it helps couples understand if they are fulfilled in their current relationship, identify gaps that need to be bridged and equitably divide partnership responsibilities. In the podcast, Jennifer discussed three key choices that couples face as they combine their parallel lives and build a shared life together.

The first occurs early in the relationship when both partners are also relatively new to the workforce. Several external events such as upcoming nuptials or career opportunities involving relocation present unexplored challenges. What makes it more complicated for millennials is that they don't have many relatable examples.

The previous generation chose partners differently. Today, both men and women are taking time to figure out what they want personally and professionally. They are experimenting more and marrying later. Women are also far more financially independent than before. Together these factors create an ambiguous situation with several unknowns.

The second major choice is during the middle of one's career. That is when it is less about external events and more about asking our inner selves if we have met our personal and professional goals. At this stage, people tend to ask themselves whether their 25 years old selves will be happy with the way life turned out for them.

This mid-life crisis can be unsettling for both partners even if they did well early in their careers. It turns out that those who followed someone else's dream or spent their entire youth building up an insurance for the future tend to have professional regrets that wreak havoc on their personal lives.

In the third critical juncture, couples confront the question of what remains after mid career goals have been achieved and there aren't shared projects to look forward to. That is when couples either disengage with each other or renew their partnership. Those who disengage think that it is too late for change and those who renew, attempt to build a new life together with different goals.

In the years to come, there might be an additional decision that couples have to grapple with—how to handle feeling like a millennial after the age of 60 years. Authors of *The 100-Year Life— Living and Working in an Age of Longevity*, Lynda Gratton and Andrew Scott suggest that people have a real shot at living up to or more than 100 years of age. At the same time, lifespan of companies will shrink and the whole concept of retirement will cease to exist.

This means that being a millennial will be redefined. In addition to altering the nature of workplaces, the 100-year life phenomena might also change dating and marriage. We are already seeing signs of this with the emergence of hundreds of age agnostic dating platforms and communities.

The conventional wisdom regarding dating and marriage is that couples struggle to begin with and eventually figure things out. Dr Jennifer's research suggests that this approach no longer works. Relationship issues don't figure themselves out unless there is a contract or an agreement of sorts. Couples not only need to have a shared understanding of who they are and what they want but also need to recontract before every major transition.

Dr Jennifer and Gianpiero crafted such an agreement 15 years ago on a warm summer evening in Sicily, and thus far, it has served them well. Leveraging their relationship contract, they dealt with several ups and downs as a team, including a time when Dr Jennifer almost gave up her career.

Drafting a contract or having a shared understanding of the contours of relationships may not be enough to make things work but not making the effort can spell doom for dual-career couples.

Key Takeaways

- Key to relationship bliss for dual-career couples is a psychological contract of sorts.
- The relationship contract is a description of the kind of life a couple wants to build together.
- Relationship issues don't figure themselves out unless there is a contract or an agreement of sorts.
- Couples need to have a shared understanding of who they are and what they want.
- They also need to recontract before every major transition.

PART 4

AUGMENTING
PERSONAL
PRODUCTIVITY

CHAPTER 41

THE POWER OF COMPOUNDING

Most of us start a new year by setting ambitious goals to reinvent ourselves; that is the easy part. By 8th January, one week from the start of the year, 25 per cent of new year resolutions fall apart. And by the time the year ends, we break 90 per cent of our resolutions and fall back into the same old routines and rituals.

We fail to achieve most of our goals because behavioural change is hard, especially when we are busy, stressed and distracted—the default work mode for many millennials. There are six practical ideas that can help us commit to our new year resolutions.

First, instead of trying to change all habits at once, we should focus on one habit and work towards micro-improvements. Upon analysing all the years I failed to fulfil my new year resolutions, I realized that I wanted to change too much too soon. In her book *Presence*, a psychologist at Harvard Business School, Dr Amy Cuddy, advocates for 'self-nudging', a process of constantly setting small goals in place of large ones.

Instead of aspiring to be a new person by March, I should have followed the advice of *Atomic Habits* author James Clear, and focused on becoming one per cent better every day. Micro-improvements compound over time to deliver incredible results.

Last year, I wanted to read more research papers and connect with more scientists in different fields. To make that happen, I committed to reading a page a day. Initially I found it challenging but this daily habit helped me meaningfully connect with hundreds of top researchers around the world.

Second, add friction and make it difficult to continue practicing bad habits. One new year resolution that fell apart for me last year was not being able to take guilt free breaks from technology. I found it impossible to switch off and often kept twiddling on my phone late at night. I realized that I was obsessively checking my emails and notifications only because my phone was around. I had allowed my attention to be hacked.

From the last week of December, I have been charging my phone in the living room at night. While it is too early to celebrate success, my screen time has reduced and I have been sleeping much better. By making it slightly more difficult to check my phone at night, I have enhanced my sleep quality and implicitly, my overall productivity.

The reverse of this is also true. When we wish to pursue a good habit, we must make it impossible to ignore and easy to follow.

Third, focus on the process and behaviour, not the end result. Most of our new year resolutions are framed by negativity. We tend to course correct things we dislike about ourselves—say our weight, attention span, Netflix binging habits, etc.—and they can demotivate us even before we get started.

Specific goals are important, but they don't deliver results by themselves. Mason Currey, the author of *Daily Rituals: How Artists Work* analysed daily routines of creative geniuses in art, music and literature and concluded that almost all of them had elaborate rituals and routines that propelled them to meet their goals. The key insight for all of us is that the success or failure of new year resolutions strongly correlates with our habits.

Fourth, warm up. Unless we start making subtle changes to our habits and rituals 4–6 weeks in advance, 1st January will turn out to be just like any other day. A head start towards our new year resolution also allows us to experiment, tinker and fail without feeling too guilty.

Fifth, find a peer coach to track your resolutions. Being accountable to someone pushes us to be consistent with our efforts.

This New Year's Eve, some of our community members met for breakfast to share their resolutions and find peers pursuing similar or complementary goals. I noticed that the pursuit of finding a coach further strengthened commitment to follow through on resolutions.

Lastly, keep the deeper purpose of your resolution in mind. While most new year resolutions are about body health and external signalling, the ones that actually work have a clear sense of why. There will be days when things go awry and we feel like abandoning our resolutions. Remembering the purpose underlying our resolution will give us the strength to push through.

Let's try and take a habit-centric approach to our resolutions for the year 2020. Progress is a great motivational force. By taking pride in consistent micro-improvements, we will be setting ourselves and our communities for success.

Key Takeaways

- Strive to become one per cent better every day.
- Add friction to your bad habits.
- Focus on the process and learn to enjoy it.
- Warm up.
- Find a peer coach for accountability.
- Remember your 'why'.

CHAPTER 42

OVERCOMING FOBO AND FOMO

Fifteen years ago, investor and podcast host, Patrick McGinnis wrote a column for *Harbus*, the student newspaper of Harvard Business School where he identified two potent forces guiding decision-making for the entire student body: fear of missing out (FOMO) and fear of a better option (FOBO). Then McGinnis graduated and forgot about it—until a New York Times reporter looking into the origins of FOMO and FOBO, tracked it back to him.

With the help of Patrick's masterclass on networkcapital.tv, I have trained myself to negotiate better with FOBO. FOBO, also referred to as maximization, is the relentless pursuit of all possible options for fear that we will miss out on the 'best' outcome. This wild goose chase leads to indecision, fatigue, stress and regret.

FOBO is a by-product of our hyper-busy, hyper-connected world filled with possibilities we can't ignore. Most of life is about freedom to choose but freedom left unchecked, having choices can make us prisoners of our own mind. Bill Schwarz's research shows that up till a certain point, happiness increases with the number of choices and then plummets with vigorous pace.

As Network Capital grew from being a small skill sharing platform to a large, global community, I realized that FOBO was weighing me down. By trying to maximize every outcome, I became indecisive and took several sub-optimal decisions. It adversely affected my motivation and pushed me to solve problems that didn't exist. I got so busy trying to solve inconsequential problems that I didn't have the bandwidth to attend to issues critical for my most important stakeholders.

Patrick explains that when we have FOBO (and particularly when we combine it with FOMO), our decision-making paralysis turns into FODA (Fear of Doing Anything).

Dwight Eisenhower, the 34th President of the United States, famously said that the most urgent decisions are rarely the most important ones. The Eisenhower Matrix has four components, which we can use to grapple with the spectre of FOBO:

1. *Important, but not urgent:* We can decide when to do such tasks. I often put such activities on my calendar and try to finish them off in one sitting.
2. *Urgent and important:* These are the tasks that require both focus and creativity. They also need to be attended to immediately. That is why I prioritize them over everything else.
3. *Urgent but not important:* These should be delegated to someone else. The cost of wasting your time on such tasks is far more than the cost of outsourcing it. I do such tasks usually on my way back from work as I deal with the torturous Delhi traffic.
4. *Not important and not urgent:* These things should be postponed without guilt. I have learned to ignore such tasks.

The Eisenhower matrix made me realize that it is impossible to manage time. Considering all tasks as equally important and spreading them through the day is a sure shot recipe for disaster. Instead we need to focus on managing our energy and attention on high-stake decisions. Seems intuitive, right? Then why don't more people follow it?

FOBO, FOMO and FODA together make a deadly combination, one that can only be mitigated by ruthless prioritization. These days everyone is burned out: millennials, baby boomers, corporate folks, start-up leaders and even primary school students. Everyone seems to be talking about work-life balance without getting to the core of the issue.

The truth of the matter is that we are burned out not because we are doing more work but because we are exhausting ourselves taking inconsequential decisions that seem urgent.

Now my personal productivity is all about ignoring the urgent and focusing on the important stuff that moved the needle. It required deliberate practice, patience and rigorous commitment to the Eisenhower matrix. Many times, I was tempted by the charms of FOBO, but I resisted and stuck it out.

By spending almost no time on low-stake, urgent decisions, I carved out more time for my family and for travelling, reading, writing, working and relaxing. Among other things, I have learned the art of being productive without being busy.

Key Takeaways
- FOMO + FOBO + FODA = Burnout
- Never mistake urgent for important and vice versa.
- The key to greater productivity and creativity is ruthless prioritization.
- More decisions almost always mean bad decisions.
- Spend most of your time on high-stake and important things. Let the little things go. They are not worth your time.

CHAPTER 43

WHY TOO MUCH SELF-REFLECTION CAN BE BAD FOR YOU

As someone who reflects a fair bit and writes a daily journal, I found organizational psychologist Tasha Eurich's study on self-reflection deeply unnerving. I was confident her results would show that people who introspect would have a clearer understanding of themselves and their workplace. It turns out that people who scored high on self-reflection were more stressed, less satisfied with their jobs and relationships, more self-absorbed and they felt less in control of their lives. Given the facts at hand, I wondered if I should stop reflecting?

According to World Economic Forum, emotional intelligence, empathy, influence, persuasion, communication and collaboration are among the most important skills for the 21st century. All of them stem from self-awareness but data suggests that 95 per cent of people believe that they're self-aware, but only about 10–15 per cent actually are. A University of Sydney psychologist, Anthony Grant, says that there is no relationship between introspection and insight. When we introspect, our response is similar to a hungry cat watching mice. We eagerly pounce on half-baked insights without questioning their validity or value. Clearly there is something wrong with the way we are reflecting.

Tasha Eurich defines self-awareness unicorns as those that were rated high in self-awareness (both by themselves and by others). She put together a group of 50 such unicorns who had started out with only low to moderate self-awareness. On analysing their speech patterns and interview transcripts, she found that unicorns reported asking 'what' often and 'why' rarely. In fact, the word 'why' appeared less than 150 times, but the word 'what' appeared more than 1,000 times.

If we want to build our introspection muscles and make reflection work for us, we need to repivot from 'why' to 'what'. Asking why traps us into the past and makes us victims of the operating context. Framing the same question by asking 'what', helps us take ownership of our problems. Also, it enables us to zoom out and analyse what happened, with an objective lens.

This is obviously easier said than done but is surely worth a try. If we didn't get a promotion or a raise we really wanted, asking ourselves why won't reveal much. It is often beyond our sphere of influence. Instead of that, if we try and figure out what we can do to get it next time, is far more helpful.

In one of my professional roles, I managed sales for large public sector enterprises. My team was composed of three more people who had far more experience and expertise than myself. I felt they were going out of their way to make things hard for me. They would cancel meetings last minute and invite me for negotiations knowing fully well that I was out of town attending to a different customer. For the first six months, I kept asking myself why and got nowhere. Then I repivoted and tried to figure what I could do to win their trust and make a functional team.

The what-centric reflection enabled me to see my blind spots. Without giving enough time to understand how they worked, I had waltzed in with my business school frameworks and strategies. I hadn't paid enough emphasis on the fact that I was much younger, far less experienced but more senior in terms of organizational hierarchy. Only after talking about the elephant in the room and accepting my shortcomings did we start coming closer as a team. I took Tasha Eurich's advice and asked them—what do I do that most annoys you. It was hard but I saw the dynamics of our relationship change. Over the course of time, one of the team members even mentored me and offered precious advice on dealing with tricky customers. Together we went on to win some large deals and I learned that happiness and job satisfaction is not a solitary pursuit.

Almost every day there is a new study on happiness. Far from confirming that 'happiness comes from within,' a wide body of research tells us almost the exact opposite. *Our happiness depends on other people.*

What-centric reflection propels our happiness and overall satisfaction. That is why it is essential that when we reflect, we focus on our actions and try to empower the people who matter to us the most and those we spend most of our time with. Our journey towards self-awareness is both communal and incremental. We can't become more self-aware by ourselves and we won't wake up drastically more self-aware tomorrow. We should just aim for micro-improvements over a period of time and have the courage to embark upon that journey.

Key Takeaways

- Ninety-five per cent of people believe that they're self-aware, but only about 10–15 per cent are.
- There is no relationship between introspection and insight.
- If we want to make reflection work for us, we need to repivot from 'why' to 'what'.
- Our happiness depends on other people.
- Our journey towards self-awareness is both communal and incremental.

CHAPTER 44

WHEN DO MILLENNIALS WORK?

According to a report by Visual Capitalist, 188 million emails, 42 million WhatsApp messages and 18.1 million texts are sent out every minute. This speck of time allows for 4.5 million YouTube videos, 4.8 million GIFs, 1.4 million tinder swipes, one million Facebook logins, 3.8 million Google searches and 0.4 million mobile app downloads. Taking a yearly count makes things even more intimidating—100 trillion emails are sent every year.

We spend close to 0.7 million hours watching Netflix every minute, a 300 per cent increase from last year. India is one of the fastest growing consumer of internet markets with millennials redefining digital consumption trends. We now have a new category of broadcasting applications blitz scaling across India. Each time I open new age 'vlogging' apps millennials seem to be broadcasting short videos of what they are up to. Activities include dancing, rapping, chilling and believe it or not, napping. I am glad that millennials across the country are coming online but the puzzling cyber behaviour and digital engagement makes me wonder—when do millennials actually work?

By work, I don't mean attending meetings, providing status updates and replying to chats and emails. These tasks fall under the category of shallow work: stuff that can get done with wavering attention and doesn't really move the needle.

Deep work is characterized by tasks that require more cognitive resources, creativity and undisturbed focus. Deep work makes us productive and creates conditions for long-term success. Almost all personal and professional growth is a direct result of deep work. Shallow work, on the other hand, gives us the illusion of being busy, saps creativity and leaves us exhausted. Being busy has nothing to do with being productive. Today, it is possible to be very busy, put in copious hours of work and still not create anything of consequence.

It is no secret that if we want to excel in any field, we need to go above and beyond the bare minimum effort required to hold on to our jobs. Does it mean that we expand our to-do list, network more and take on more responsibilities? Not necessarily. In fact, doing so can seriously backfire if timing, effort and organizational priorities are misaligned. We can be as busy as we like but if we are not adding value to the most critical goals of our organization, we are wasting everyone's time.

Productivity is output divided by input. Therefore, being productive means getting more done with less. Because time is finite and our lives keep getting busier, the only way to be consistently more productive is to sharpen focus.

Focus is not binary. It isn't something we either have or not. Like every good habit, focus needs discipline and is slowly built over a period of time. Expecting to wake up one fine day with renewed focus and determination is a sure shot way to fail.

To write this chapter, I interviewed 12 super productive Network Capital community members working in fields characterized by a constant flux of new information: high frequency trading, journalism and social media analytics. I was curious how they managed to get deep work done despite the profound digital cacophony in their industries.

It turns out that almost all my interviewees had five common traits. First, they knew their most productive hours and blocked them for undisturbed deep work. Most of them also told their friends, colleagues and family members in order to set low expectations about the response time during that period. Second, they focused on doing one thing at a time. Not one of them multi-tasked. Third, they took guilt free breaks from technology. Fourth, they built great work habits. Many even had elaborate work rituals. Fifth, they felt comfortable saying no, something I always struggle to do.

In essence, if want to be more productive and creative, we can't afford to be in the perennial respond and react mode. Being a millennial, I understand FOMO and the constant need to be on top of things. That said, it is time to transform FOMO to JOMO (joy of missing out) and commit to carving time for deep work.

Key Takeaways

- Focus is not binary. Like every good habit, it is slowly built over a period of time.
- Learn to differentiate between deep and shallow work.
- Your productivity and creativity depend on your deep work.
- Take guilt free breaks from technology.
- There is joy in missing out.
- Get to the bottom of things. Being on top of everything is not required.

CHAPTER 45

THE HARD WORK DELUSION

Hard work has always been romanticized but never as much as it is today. Social media is plastered with quotes along the lines of 'You can't out-work me' or 'Sleep is for the weak'. People take great pride in flaunting their punishing work routines, torturous keto diets and robot-like well-being rituals. We have gamified the experience of being human and fail to see the profound irony. If only hard work could fix it!

Romantic proclamations of hard work are distracting and debilitating for almost everyone involved. Let's explore why. First, they confuse being busy with being effective. Second, they unintentionally standardize aspirations. Third and most important, they make it seem like pivoting or changing the course of action is a sign of weakness.

Hard work and success are most certainly correlated but correlation is not causation. I have been a part of several global communities like Network Capital, Global Shapers and UNLEASH. Upon analysing the highest performers among these communities, I can safely say that their informed and intelligent choices were the real catalysts of success. Hard work helped but only because they chose wisely.

Arriving at the right set of choices needs robust mental models and intentional experimentation. Unfortunately, the incentive structures in schools, colleges and most workplaces are antithetical to calculated experiments and evidence-based decision-making. They are designed to help us improve without questioning the underlying framework of evaluation. Instead of encouraging us to change tracks in face of evidence or design frameworks that work for us, they nudge us into a weird competitive game with ourselves and our peers. Peter Thiel's quote strongly resonates with me—'Competition is for losers'.

If you are trying very hard and find yourself uninspired and exhausted, you are most likely playing the wrong game. No matter how many hours you put in, things won't change.

According to a World Economic Forum report, 85 per cent of the jobs of the year 2030 don't exist yet. No one really knows what sectors and industries will be in vogue but it is obvious that following trends and mindsets of the past will be foolhardy.

Instead of chasing and competing on buzzwords and fashionable acronyms in tech, if we focus on understanding our strengths, weaknesses, inclinations and motivations, we would do a far greater service to ourselves and to the society at large. Armed with more self-awareness and an open mind, we will be able to frame more intelligent questions and hopefully design systems that can address pressing challenges with an innovative approach.

I feel that time has come for us to ignore impassioned proclamations of hard work and focus more on picking the right problems to solve. Let's begin by stating the obvious—sleep is not for the weak and working hard for the heck of it is a waste of time and potential.

Key Takeaways

- Being busy and being effective are different things.
- Learning to pick the right problems is far more important than the time spent on solving them.
- Arriving at the right set of choices needs robust mental models and intentional experimentation.
- Competition is for losers.

PART 5

LEARNING FROM
THE BEST

CHAPTER 46

THE POMODORO TECHNIQUE

On an average we work for 80,000 hours over our lifetime. Assuming we sleep for eight hours a day, this translates to 1,000 minutes that are theoretically available to work, better ourselves, spend time with friends and family, exercise, explore and indulge.

Let's divide these 1,000 minutes into 25-minute segments. Why? Because of one of the simplest and most practical attention management techniques is called the Pomodoro method. It is based on the simple premise that short bursts of focused work sprints are far better for productivity and creativity than long, distracted work marathons.

Pomodoro means tomato in Italian and this technique owes its name to the tomato shaped timer that buzzes after 25 minutes. The Pomodoro method has six straightforward steps.

1. Figure out what needs to be done in the 25-minute sprint.
2. Set the pomodoro timer.
3. Work on the task without distraction.
4. Finish your work sprint.
5. Take a short (usually five minutes) break.
6. After four 25-minute sprints, take a longer break (15–30 minutes).

Now let's get back to the 1,000 minutes a day. We have 40 slots of 25 minutes each. How should we spend them?

There are no standard answers to such questions but they often come down to priorities, goals and knowledge of our own selves: How do we want to relax, who do we want to spend time with, how might we prepare for our future aspirations, how should one say no, etc.

We will now be exploring the routines and rituals of some of the most creative people in the world. You don't need to follow what they do blindly. These are just meant to serve as examples and reference points. The truth of the matter is that you need to design your days, weeks, months and years to accomplish what matters most to you. In the process, you will understand your raison d'être (reason for being).

You might realize that working in 25-minute sprints isn't that hard. Figuring out what to work on, why and with whom takes far more energy and time.

There are two parts to what makes a creative genius: immersion and improvisation. Immersion comes from rituals and routines and improvisation comes from losing oneself in the moment. For that, one needs a quiet, calm and peaceful mind that is present. I feel Pomodoro method is a simple method to make it happen.

I have always been curious to explore how some people are able to get so much done in one day. In the upcoming chapters we will discuss the daily routines and rituals of top performers in different fields. As we explore the routines of those we admire, let's find out how they divided their 1,000 minutes every day. Further, let's see what are some recurring commonalities.

CHAPTER 47

PAUL GRAHAM

Computer scientist and co-founder of seed accelerator, *Y Combinator*, Paul Graham divides his day into two parts—one where he follows what he calls the maker schedule and the other where he is on a manager schedule.

Essentially a maker is a creator of content, code or community. She needs undisturbed blocks of time to get something meaningful done. That is why procedural meetings can have a negative spill over effect on the entire day of a maker.

A manager on the other hand, at least by conventional standards, needs to attend meetings, respond, react and fight fires that might disrupt day-to-day work. None of us is strictly one or the other. We need to do both, make and manage.

Back in the 1990s when Paul first became an entrepreneur, he used to code from dinner time till about 3:00 am every day as he did not want to get interrupted. Thereafter he would sleep till 11:00 am. He would then come to office around noon and stay till dinner time managing day-to-day business operations. In effect he had two workdays each day, one on the manager's schedule and one on the maker's schedule.

Even today as the head of one of the world's most prestigious accelerators, his work and attention distribution has a similar rhythm. He needs to advise hundreds of start-up founders who are on the maker's schedule without taking them out of their state of flow.

He has hacked the system he devised by simulating the manager's schedule within the maker's schedule via the office hours. Several times a week he sets aside a chunk of time to meet the founders *Y Combinator* has funded. These blocks of time are reserved at the end of his working day and since founders sign up for them voluntarily, they must see value in it.

To a certain degree, we have tried to institutionalize this on Network Capital. After creating thousands of mentor-matches around the world, the biggest realization for me was that everyone—no matter how busy or famous—has 15 minutes to spare if those 15 minutes are slotted appropriately.

Without taking time out to 'make', there will be nothing left for us to 'manage'.

CHAPTER 48

HARUKI MURAKAMI

Former jazz bar operator turned best-selling author who took to writing inspired by a baseball match, Murakami is quite unlike the protagonist of his critically acclaimed work *Norwegian Wood*. There the protagonist spends most of his time smoking cigarettes, reading and listening to records while in real life Murakami is quite the epitome of discipline and routine.

When Murakami is in the writing mode for a novel (which is often as he writes a new book every 3–4 years), he gets up at 4:00 am and works for almost six hours straight. In the afternoon, he runs for 10 km or swims a mile (often both). Thereafter he reads and listens to some music. Jazz remains his favourite since the time he used to run a jazz bar in Tokyo. Murakami goes to bed at 9:00 pm.

He sticks to this routine every day without variation. Murakami is a big proponent of routines and rituals. He calls it a form of mesmerizing that helps reach a deeper state of mind.

To do this consistently for six months to a year (the time it takes him to finish a novel), he confesses the need for substantial mental and physical strength, much like during running (his other love). Murakami says that physical strength is as necessary as artistic sensitivity. His strength has always been the fact that he works hard and can handle a lot physically. As he puts it, 'I'm more of a workhorse than a racehorse.'

The source of Murakami's creative genius may or may not be rigorous discipline but it surely augments it. Although he was always a 'workhorse', his creative genius flowered when he traded his jazz bar for a sheath of writing paper and a fountain pen, and his smoking habit for running shoes. To be clear, he didn't forget jazz. It is still an integral part of where his inspiration to write comes from.

Subtle changes in lifestyle design can unleash bursts of creativity that put us in a state of flow. And with flow, the trials and tribulations of committing to a regimented routine transform into the joy of meaningful rituals.

CHAPTER 49

MAYA ANGELOU

Maya Angelou was one of America's greatest authors and poets who enabled millions of readers to better understand nuances of identity, racism and family. Her genius stemmed from consistency and religious commitment to her routine.

She was an early riser and usually started her day at 05:30 am. After her morning coffee with her husband, she would head to work. Office for her was a tiny hotel room where she kept a dictionary, a Bible, a deck of cards and a bottle of sherry.

She began her work day around 07:00 am and would work non-stop till noon. On a non-productive day she would go on till 12:30 pm. Angelou referred to this time for deep work as lonely and marvellous.

She would come home around 02:00 pm and read through her work. Then she took a break, showered and prepared dinner. This was her time to zoom out and try to not think about work. She would conclude the day with a drink with her husband.

We often hear the phrase 'writer's block' that roughly means the period of time where writers are unable to make creative progress. Upon analysing the habits of creative people, one theme that keeps recurring is that great artists don't wait for inspiration. They nurture it by commitment to their craft. That is why the next time you are finding it hard to build, write or create, remember that even on a bad day, Angelou wrote without getting distracted for over 5 hours.

CHAPTER 50

YUVAL NOAH HARARI

Yuval Noah Harari is a historian, philosopher and the bestselling author of *Sapiens: A Brief History of Humankind*, *Homo Deus: A Brief History of Tomorrow* and *21 Lessons for the 21st Century*. His books have sold over 23 million copies worldwide and he is perhaps the man asking the best questions about our past and how it relates to an uncertain future where governments, technology companies and civil society seem to be clueless about figuring out a sustainable model for cooperation.

One of his biggest fears is that with the mainstreaming of AI and technological disruption, machines and algorithms will know us far better than we know ourselves. We seem to be at peace letting our most precious resource—our attention—get hacked by targeted cat videos and violent political campaigns. All of us seem to be getting louder so much so that it is impossible to hear our inner voice.

To steer clear of all this cacophony and to have the spiritual energy to think about the world at large, Harari lives a life without a smartphone. He meditates for two hours every day and takes two months off every year to meditate in India.

He does not read the newspaper or skim through clickbait content. Harari is known to pick up books and read them cover to cover. It seems like he is not in a rush to be on top of things. He says that he isn't a journalist or a politician so his goal is to get to the bottom of things, instead of constantly thinking about pithy replies and be in the respond-and-react mode.

All of us don't need to literally follow Harari's schedule but we can learn three key lessons from him.

First, take time out every day to disconnect. You could go for a run; you could write or play an instrument or just do nothing. Any activity where the pursuit is the goal, works. This time to recharge and think is precious if we want to become better thinkers.

Second, buy time. Harari creates time for deep work by prioritizing important over urgent. He has a team for research, social media, speaking engagements and business partnerships. We may not be able to live without a smart phone like Harari or afford a team to work for us, but we can learn from his core idea of creating undisturbed blocks of time to focus on work that moves the needle.

Third, get to know yourself. You may or may not like what you discover by thinking about your inner self but it is an important exercise. There is not one fixed true self of a person. Long-term professional growth requires us to take time and energy to figure out the epicentre of our wanton desires, needs and behaviours.

CHAPTER 51

RICHARD FEYNMAN

Richard P. Feynman was arguably one of the most brilliant, iconoclastic and influential minds of the post-war generation. Albert Einstein presided over Feynman's first seminar as a graduate student and was moved. Bill Gates was so inspired by his pedagogy that he called Feynman, 'the greatest teacher I never had'. His work helping understand the interaction of light and matter earned him a Nobel Prize in the year 1965.

Known for his knack of combining different strands of knowledge and explaining complex concepts with wit and clarity, Feynman redefined how people thought about physics. When he wasn't researching particle physics, he was writing, dabbling in the arts, sketching or playing the bongo.

A Cornell University professor, Samuel Bacharach, shared five elements of Feynman's productivity and creativity.

First, don't worry about perceptions. Feynman was motivated by the discovery of truth. Other people's opinions didn't distract him. It is worth noting that he was immensely popular with most of his students and peers. It seems like the less he cared about perceptions, the more favourably he was perceived.

Second, don't think about what you want to be. Think about what you want to do.

'Fall in love with some activity, and do it!' Feynman advised.

> Nobody ever figures out what life is all about, and it doesn't matter. Explore the world. Nearly everything is really interesting if you go into it deeply enough. Work as hard and as much as you want to on the things you like to do the best. Don't think about what you want to be, but what you want to do. Keep up some kind of a minimum with other things so that society doesn't stop you from doing anything at all.

The larger lesson I took from this quote was that one should spend far more time on inputs than on musings about outcomes that are, in many cases, beyond our control.

Third, stop trying to be a know-it-all. Knowing what you don't know is wisdom and figuring out how to learn it is intelligence. After he became the CEO of Microsoft, Satya Nadella said that being a learn-it-all connotes a growth mindset, essential for both innovation and culture change. Even when we get recognition for our work, it is important to have a hungry mind and hungry heart.

Fourth, get off the computer. 'There is a computer disease,' Feynman tells us. 'Anybody who works with computers knows about [it]. It's a very serious disease and it interferes completely with the work. The trouble with computers is that you 'play' with them!'

It is interesting that Feynman spoke of digital detox back in the day when there were no mobiles and social media.

Fifth, have a sense of humour. One of my favourite Feynman lines is, 'The first principle is that you must not fool yourself—and you are the easiest person to fool.'

In addition to understanding his work principles, let us now dive into his iconic mental model tool to convey complicated information concisely. It is now popularly called *The Feynman Technique*.

This is the four-step process you can apply to learn quickly and efficiently.

1. **Identify what you want to learn**
   This boils down to writing down key questions you have about the subject or topic.

2. **Teach it to a child**
   If you can teach a concept to a child, you understand it. If you can't, you don't.

   Write down everything you know about the subject. The key is to write simply in a way that a child can understand. Obviously, the idea is not to dumb down content or be simplistic in our approach. The goal is to remove the fluff and jargon. You also need to be brief. Children have a small attention span so you need to train yourself to convey what you want without inflicting unnecessary words.

3. **Identify your knowledge gaps**
   This is when you understand the known and unknown, unknowns. Addressing these knowledge gaps sets us on the path to truly understanding a subject.

4. **Organize your thoughts and tell a story or teach someone**
   'All things are made of atoms—little particles that move around in perpetual motion, attracting each other when they are a little distance apart, but repelling upon being squeezed into one another.'

With this sentence, even if you don't understand anything about physics, you will vividly remember that everything is made up of atoms. In one sentence, Feynman explains the foundational existence of our universe both to a child and a physics expert.

CHAPTER 52

NAVAL RAVIKANT

Naval Ravikant is the founder of AngelList, a platform that is democratizing venture investing, and an early investor in Twitter and Uber. Every time you hail an Uber cab, Naval makes about 0.1 per cent of the fare. In addition to his success in business and investing, Naval has become a guide and philosopher for the ambitious young millennials around the world through his blogs and podcasts. His intellectual appeal spans political and economic spectrums, and his genius lies in the fact that he can meaningfully engage with and learn from those who disagree with him.

He is one of the clearest thinkers and communicators in the business world. I think he owes his success to his radical honesty, first-principle thinking and ruthless prioritizing. Naval guards his time carefully even though in his own words he is a tad lazy and not a particularly hard worker. His success is yet another proof that what we choose to work on and with whom is perhaps the strongest indicator of future success.

Naval is famous for saying that you should be too busy to *do coffee*, while still keeping an uncluttered calendar. As someone who passionately dislikes non-transactional meetings, Naval keeps a large chunk of his day for thinking, reflecting and being present in the moment. By spending time with his thoughts without distraction and focusing on what he controls—the present moment—he is able to outthink others. Success in business and in life doesn't come from working a little more than others. It comes from having the ability to both zoom out and zoom in to see the larger picture and also the unobvious intricacies.

He doesn't have a typical day or a typical week as he considers it to be at odds with this quest for freedom. Naval aspires to do the work he cares about, be productive (not because he needs to but because he values time), spend time with family and read. He calls himself a conscious bookworm and spends an hour before bed-time, reading. I learnt that he doesn't take notes or underlines text as it takes him away from the present moment.

As you might have guessed, his way of networking is doing interesting things. People flock towards those who have something original to say and have unique value to add. Naval certainly does.

CHAPTER 53

SUSAN CAIN

Susan Cain is the author of the bestsellers *Quiet Power: The Secret Strengths of Introverts* and *Quiet: The Power of Introverts in A World That Can't Stop Talking*, which has been translated into 40 languages; is in its seventh year on the New York Times best seller list; and was named the number one best book of the year by *Fast Company* magazine, which also named Cain as one of its *Most Creative People* in business.

After spending more than 10 years studying and working in the field of law, Cain had to repivot her career. It turned out to be a blessing in disguise. As it happened, one of the senior partners in the law firm she worked at walked into her office and told her that she would not be making partner in the stipulated time. This was all she had worked for, so, understandably it came as a shock. Tears followed. At her lowest point she stumbled into clarity: She never cared about law. Writing was what she wanted to pursue.

Soon after she enrolled in New York University's (NYU) evening programme for writing and embarked upon a journey that transformed her and made her the icon for embracing quiet and solitude.

She does not think her corporate career was a waste. In fact, she credits her long-drawn law stint for enabling her to understand how the world works, appreciate and critique the way humans engage with each other in groups and for providing her with the financial security required to pursue her creative endeavours without worry.

Even though her savings at the time she quit law were not significant, the training empowered her to monetize her skills like negotiation, while she figured her path as a writer.

Susan has an awe-inspiring work ethic, something we can all learn from. After spending the first 90 minutes of her day with family, she heads to a café to work without interruption for almost 4 hours. Being a coffee afficionado, she rewards her deep work with a piping hot cup of latte. Such mornings are when she gets most of her creative work done.

Thereafter she takes an hour to answer emails using a technique called batching. Instead of frequently interrupting their work and replying to chats and emails, many creative people like Susan have dedicated time for emails and correspondence.

Post-lunch, Cain allocates 2–3 hours to media interviews, meetings, podcasts, etc. This is her time dedicated to sharing her work with the wider world and also strengthening her ideas by engaging with people.

The secret to Cain's productivity is to plan things in a way that she has undisturbed chunks of time for her family and for her work. This empowers her to be in a state of flow and bring her best to the things that matter the most.

Susan Cain's work life explains how productivity and creativity essentially boil down to priority.

CHAPTER 54

BRENÉ BROWN

Dr Brené Brown is a social worker turned research professor at the University of Houston and also a visiting professor of management at the University of Texas at Austin McCombs School of Business.

She has spent the past two decades studying courage, vulnerability, shame and empathy and is the author of five number one New York Times bestsellers, namely, *The Gifts of Imperfection*, *Daring Greatly*, *Rising Strong*, *Braving the Wilderness*, and her latest book, *Dare to Lead*, which is the culmination of a seven-year study on courage and leadership.

Dr Brown's TED Talk—The Power of Vulnerability—is one of the top five most viewed TED Talks in the world with over 45 million views. She is also the first researcher to have a filmed lecture on Netflix.

Dr Brown's success comes from chasing her curiosity, not expectations. Her 20s were largely unremarkable, at least academically. She got her college degree at the age of 29 and by her own account exhausted her 30s trying to perfect, prove and perform. One of the most useful career advice she offers is to pick the right problems to solve. Hard work won't make you win if you are on the wrong track and competing against your curiosity and conviction. She says that we should make sure that when it comes to being successful, your ladder is leaning against the right building.

It was only in her 40s that all her experiences came together. She became the illustrious academic-cum-vulnerability champion after an Oprah interview and a viral TED Talk. She built a thriving business from her coaching and speaking engagements.

While all the professional success was welcome, it proved to highlight the dichotomy between Dr Brown's ambition and her reluctant relationship with being a public figure, between the scholar who preaches vulnerability and the one who's built a wall of protection against the outside world. She is still figuring out this conundrum but so far, she has prioritized her mission to share her lessons and findings for the benefit of the wider world over her discomfort of constantly being in the public gaze.

If there is one phrase that we should remember from Dr Brown's research, this is it—choose courage over comfort and remember that vulnerability builds trust. Vulnerability of course doesn't mean invasion of privacy. Dr Brown is strict about setting boundaries. While she'll share what's vulnerable in her life, she makes it a point to never share what's intimate in her life.

After getting 8–9 hours of sleep Dr Brown's mornings usually start at 06:30 am with gratitude practice. It sounds something like 'I am thankful for another day and I'm going to choose courage over comfort today.' While this might seem like a small thing, it has turned out to be a purpose reinforcing ritual that kickstarts her day on a high.

After a light breakfast and some exercise, she gets to work. Being an introvert, she takes at least half a day every week just to be with herself and think. As someone who loves swimming and walking, she loves to digitally detox without guilt. I deliberately used the word guilt here as Dr Brown constantly reminds us that guilt is

'I did something bad' whereas shame is 'I am something bad'. Shame is focused on self and guilt is focused on behaviour.

When it comes to creativity and productivity hacks, one should always focus on behaviour. Dr Brown owes it to three habits she has carefully cultivated: exercise, contemplation and solitude.

CHAPTER 55

ELIZABETH GILBERT

Elizabeth Gilbert's memoir *Eat Pray Love* transformed her into a global cultural phenomenon. Thereafter she has written four more books and also delivered two wildly popular TED Talks (her first TED Talk has over 17 million views and counting). She also kept up a rigorous schedule of speaking engagements and started teaching creativity workshops. All this while dealing with the loss of her best friend turned partner, Raya, to cancer.

Among other things, Gilbert has fascinating advice on shaping careers and writing effectively.

She suggests that there are four elements that we need to treat separately: hobby, job, career and vocation. In her twenties, as she tried to get her writing published, she worked as a bartender, a waitress and an au pair. She didn't spend much and dedicated all her remaining time to writing, which she calls her vocation and is something she loves. Even today she distinguishes between her career as a writer which depends on us, the readers, and her vocation as a writer which roughly comes down to how she feels about her own work.

She has hard-hitting and honest advice for all creatives: Nothing is owed to you. Gilbert has gone on record several times and said that creativity is not a trade. It has never been a safe bet. All one can do is to be honest to the creative process, the rigour and routine.

She has outlined a useful process for writing that includes travelling extensively to learn about different cultures and convictions, putting your work out there for critical reviews (rejections are a by-product of effort), self-forgiveness to silence your inner voice that constantly tells you that you are not good enough and of course, discipline.

When Gilbert is actively writing a book, which happens once every three or four years, her day starts at 04:30 am and she writes nonstop till mid-morning. Writing is an exhausting task that requires oodles of mental and physical labour. After the long writing session, she spends the rest of the day staring at a wall. She eats an early dinner and has an early bedtime around 07:00 or 08:00 pm. She does it all over again the next day and the next day and so on until the book is finished.

Her productivity secret is simple—be uninterrupted at your creative best for a large chunk of time. You will be surprised by how much work you can do in four hours without distractions. Gilbert guards her morning ferociously and opens up the rest of her day to the world.

She has a group of 10 friends that check-in with each other every single day. Her idea of a great night is to have early drinks or dinner with somebody she loves, come home, take a bath and read until she falls asleep. She takes two or three baths a day and considers it a big part of her wellness ritual.

What stands out about the way she works is that it is shaped on acute self-awareness. She knows herself, her creative process, her pain and her desires. This self-knowledge translates to great writing and great speaking which we all admire immensely.

CHAPTER 56

NASSIM NICHOLAS TALEB

Nassim Nicholas Taleb is currently a distinguished Professor of Risk Engineering at NYU's Tandon School of Engineering and the scientific advisor for Universa Investments. He spent 21 years as a risk taker (quantitative trader) before becoming a researcher in philosophical, mathematical and (mostly) practical problems dealing with probability. He predicted the 2008 financial crisis and alluded to the Coronavirus outbreak this year, way back in 2007 in his book *The Black Swan*.

Taleb loves to quote David Hume: 'No amount of observations of white swans can allow the inference that all swans are white, but the observation of a single black swan is sufficient to refute that conclusion.'

He owes almost all of his personal wealth and fame to being a contrarian and predicting black swan events—random, unexpected occurrences sweeping the world.

Most of us revere people who are willing to risk failure and have the gumption to bounce back from catastrophe with courage. But Taleb's example shows that there is perhaps equal if not more heroism in taking the purposeful and painful steps to prepare for the unimaginable. Not known for his restraint, sensitivity or political correctness, he tweeted in the middle of the Corona Virus crisis, 'Those who panicked early don't have to panic today.' Knowing if one is vulnerable to the volatility of accelerated damage, forms the core of Taleb's thoughts and has many applications in business and life, including our career.

While making long-term career plans, it is important to keep in mind that our forecasts are fragile and our strategies often do not take into account parameters that can create conditions akin to getting locked-in on a highway with no exit.

Whether you like him or you don't, it is worth your while to learn from his mental models, creative routine and outlook towards work.

Taleb has no faith in ambition or talent. He considers both concepts to be 'modernist nonsense'. According to him, success is about honour, feeling morally calibrated and absence of shame.

What I found most interesting about his career was how he measured up to his 20-year-old self today. He shared that he was quite happy to be judged by his 20-year-old self. Taleb takes immense pride in the fact that even though he might have swerved on occasions, he ultimately stayed in line with what he wanted to be. While he considers his maternal aunt and paternal grand uncle to be his mentors, he makes it a point to learn from the mistakes of inverse mentors: people who serve as negative examples.

It turns out that he isn't the biggest fan of routines. He says that any work done in the comfort of a routine risks being taken over by a robot.

He passionately abhors meetings and likes to have an uncluttered calendar—much like Charlie Munger and Naval Ravikant—to think, reflect, challenge and learn.

These days he wakes up very early, spends a large chunk of his time reading, teaching, thinking and writing; he eats sparsely and goes to bed at 08:00 pm. He is known to throw lavish parties for his students although I am unclear when he finds the time for them.

CHAPTER 57

CHARLIE MUNGER

Charlie Munger is one of the wealthiest and most influential businessmen in the world. He is best known as Warren Buffet's friend, business partner and the Vice Chairman of Berkshire Hathaway, perhaps the world's greatest compound interest engine, returning approximately 2,000,000 per cent on its initial value. While today we celebrate his financial success and look up to him for advice on everything from how to live a meaningful life to navigating the twists and turns of investing, his early life was actually sprinkled with challenges.

At the age of 31 years, Charlie Munger was divorced, broke and burying his nine years old son who died from cancer. Even at that moment, he did not succumb to self-pity. He worked relentlessly and trained himself out of it. Avoiding self-pity is a great way to build a competitive edge, according to Munger.

This iconic lawyer-turned-investor spends the first hour of his day learning new things and sharpening his fluency over mental models and multidisciplinary ideas shaping the world. He has trained his mind to think about problems backwards and forward, and from the lens of seemingly unrelated subjects. In his own words, 'It's made life more fun, it's made me more constructive, it has made me more helpful to others, it's made me enormously rich, you name it, that attitude really helps.'

Three principles from Munger's life explain how he has been able to function at such intensity for more than 90 years.

First, follow your curiosity. Munger says that greatest success comes in fields we are most interested in. While we can force ourselves to be reasonably good in anything, sustained excellence needs intrinsic curiosity.

Second, partner with people of high intellect, integrity and work ethic. Despite having different political views, Munger and Buffet remain close friends and business partners. Everyone they choose to partner with stands out for excellence, integrity and commitment. Such partnerships have a compounding effect and create charming win-win scenarios for everyone involved.

Third, read. The secret to Munger and Buffet's success is sitting in office and reading all day. They spend almost 80 per cent of their working day reading and thinking. Charlie Munger once famously said, 'You could hardly find a partnership in which two people settle on reading more hours of the day than in ours.'

Like most things, knowledge builds up like compound interest, one page at a time. Munger is a living example of this.

PART 6

CLARITY IS POWER: MENTAL MODELS AND THE ART OF DEEP THINKING

CHAPTER 58

OUR QUEST FOR CLARITY

Most of us go through life dealing with challenges as they emerge. We tend to be sequential in our problem-solving approach and often forget that not all problems are equal. In fact, most are best left unattended. Ignoring seemingly urgent but unimportant issues is one of the most important techniques to augment creativity and productivity. Why?

Original thinking needs an uncluttered mind. Philosopher J. Krishnamurti explains it well: 'If the mind is extraordinarily clear without a shadow of conflict, then it is really in a state of creation; it needs no expression, no fulfilment, no publicity and such nonsense.'

Unfortunately, conflict is the hallmark of our lives in the 21st century. We have problems of abundance, scarcity, conflict and most importantly, clarity.

Clarity is power and mental models are tools that propel us towards clarity. Like everything that involves power, the journey towards clarity involves struggle, self-doubt, confusion, collusion and treachery. That is why we study mental models and come up with our own tools to think through issues that hit us when we are least prepared every single day.

Broadly speaking, mental models can be categorized in the following segments:

1. Models that help augment productivity
2. Models that help us know ourselves better
3. Models that help avoid stupid mistakes
4. Models that draw upon different strands of knowledge and help uncover an 'earned secret'
5. Models that reflect upon past mistakes and uncover hidden patterns of flawed decision-making
6. Models that draw attention to important, unavoidable truths that get lost in our busy lives

While we discuss mental models in great detail, it is important that all of us develop our own examples and reference points. Today we live in a world where knowing our true selves is harder than ever. We keep swaying from pillar to post and dance to the tunes of clicks and swipes.

As we dive deep into mental models, let's ask what important truth have we learned about ourselves, the world around and the subjects that spark our curiosity. These are perhaps some of the most important questions of our time. Mental models will help, as long as we are ready to put in the effort to contextualize them.

CHAPTER 59

MIRAGES

These set of mental models help us avoid stupid mistakes by drawing attention to common errors of judgement and decision-making.

CAUSAL REDUCTIONISM

Most outcomes are products of a complex arrangement of events. There is an interwoven thread of causality that leads to a given result. However, in most cases, our minds are not able to comprehend the complexity of a situation. This leads us to a singular and reductionist understanding of events.

Popular perception is that the fourth Industrial Revolution will lead to scaled automation, rapid innovation and mass unemployment. We have painted a gloomy picture for ourselves of technological advancement at the cost of human replacement. This understanding is a typical case of Causal Reductionism. It reduces the complexity of the involved actors, events and outcomes of the fourth Industrial Revolution to the loss of existing jobs. By doing so, among other things, it ignores the possibility of creation of new industries and jobs.

Will AI lead to job losses? Of course. Are the number of jobs in the world finite? Of course not. In the years to come, we will witness a reduction in the number of institutional jobs but a massive addition of jobs where people monetize their individual stories and skills.

Similarly, in interpersonal relations and small groups, we are quick to presume that Y did X because Z happened. We superficially ascribe a 'proximate' cause. This form of thinking is most commonplace in the aftermath of a tragedy or in explaining an unusual incident. It reduces a complex chain of events into narrow fallacy. Casual Reductionism in such cases comes most prominently in the form of blame or arbitrary supposition.

To avoid Casual Reductionism, we need to sharpen our ability to think objectively and rationally. As a rule of thumb, we should, (a) Never oversimply and (b) Always look at the conjoint possibilities.

ERGODICITY

Understand the role that history (time), state (condition) and statistics together play in making decisions. For example, if you have to decide the average time it takes to bake a cake, you can either have 100 different people bake a cake at the same time or have one person bake hundred cakes. For each of the two cases the average time would not be the same. That one person baking a cake builds upon their experience of baking each time.

Systems and processes are irrevocably connected to data, numbers and patters. Therefore, our ability to make sense of the numbers and data is extremely critical. Nassim Taleb in his book *Skin in the Game* beautifully explores different methods of understanding systems and processes. One of the key principles he examines is of ergodic and non-ergodic systems.

To put it simply, ergodic systems are those which have no 'deep sense of history'. The average outcome of a sub-set is same as the outcome for the entire unit. Ergodic systems follow the same pattern across time, and return to every possible state infinite number of times.

Non-ergodic systems are those that are dynamic. They change due to multiple factors, including but not limited to—time, external stimuli, barriers, etc. Most human systems that we know are non-ergodic. This ranges from the biosphere that we live in to the iPhone 7 that we might use.

An understanding of Ergodicity is therefore extremely critical to our understanding of the world's functioning. Taleb in his book notes how policy-makers, economists, businesspersons, etc., make crucial decisions based on data. However, while doing so they tend use non-ergodic data to make future predictions. This is inherently inaccurate.

For us to avoid the pitfalls of data and to fundamentally understand systems, we must start by understanding Ergodicity. We must also understand that one system can be a combination of both ergodic and non-ergodic systems.

DUNNING–KRUGER EFFECT

The Dunning–Kruger Effect is the inability to understand one's lack of knowledge and gaps in understanding that perpetuate an illusion of superiority. A lack of metacognition (thinking about thinking) leads to a handicapped cognition (thinking). Being incompetent makes you too incompetent to recognize how incompetent you are.

Just as no one person has all the knowledge in the world, each person has something unique that only they know well. Therefore, a major part of human endeavour is to identify and refine that unique knowledge. The Dunning–Kruger Effect forms a major hurdle to the process of identification and refinement of this unique knowledge. Coined by the psychologist duo, David Dunning and Justin Kruger, the aforementioned term is a form of cognitive bias that prevents people from recognizing their own ineptness and instead creates an illusion of competence.

According to Professor Dunning,

> [t]he knowledge and intelligence that are required to be good at a task are often the same qualities needed to recognize that one is not good at that task—and if one lacks such knowledge and intelligence, one remains ignorant that one is not good at that task.

To avoid the trappings of the Dunning–Kruger Effect, reflections and metacognition are the most powerful tools. They help develop practices of self-evaluation that prevent inaccurate and inflated understanding of self.

EMERGENCE THEORY

Complex systems emerge from interaction between common, simple and relatively different elements. For example, water droplets create glaciers, each snowflake is unique in its design, neurons create consciousness etc.

The World Wide Web was developed in the 1980s. It was a global project to rapidly scale human connectivity. It had multiple actors and players involved—individuals, online service providers, governmental regulators, website creators, etc. During the 2000s, in an unanticipated turn of events, the World Wide Web lead to the emergence of a new system of 'social bookmarking' or 'tagging'. Tagging gave birth to new structures and forms of information organization and creation. For the first time in human history knowledge and information production was crowdsourced. Along with crowdsourcing, this process also organically produced a new universal language, semantics and format for tagging.

Just like the World Wide Web, there are multiple other examples of emergence in modern societies. They include the emergence of cities, economics (stock markets), language, AI, etc. In all of these cases of emergence, systems develop without a single-central organizing entity. They develop, grow and scale spontaneously.

Recognizing the working and potential of the Emergence Theory is extremely critical. Numerous businesses and companies have leveraged the phenomena's strengths to grow. Wikipedia and GitHub are the most remarkable examples of deliberate emergence.

CULTURAL PARASITISM

Ideologies are like parasites. They grow in the host's mind and modify the host's behaviour to spread to other people. Like a parasite, a successful ideology is configured to live through harsh conditions and is easy to transmit.

ABCD is a popular acronym for American Born Confused Desis, in other words, South-Asian origin American citizens. Over the last seven decades, ABCDs have created an alternative Indian culture in the United States. This alternative culture originally grew in the host minds of the parents and eventually spread to their children. Today, they are a well-known global phenomena. Massive online communities like Subtle Curry Traits have emerged in celebration of the ABCD culture.

Like ABCDs, memes are another form of Cultural Parasitism. While the two examples given are drastically different from each another, they follow the same pattern of growth and transmission. They emerged in host minds that were feeling isolated and alienated from their original cultural identities. To overcome this, they nurtured a different understanding of that original culture. By rapidly growing and spreading to other people, the newly created culture transformed into a community. This community then ensured that the parasitic culture continued to thrive. Radical religious interpretations are an extreme example of cultural parasitism.

CUMULATIVE ERROR

Error breeds error. It only takes one inaccurate statement or one false piece of information to snowball into large-scale misinformation and conspiracy theories. A networked and overly connected society exponentially increases the risks and chances of Cumulative Error.

Almost all parts of the world today follow the Gregorian calendar. Named after Pope Gregory XIII, it was introduced in the year 1582 to rectify the Cumulative Error that the Julian calendar had created. While formulating the Julian calendar, the length of the day was miscalculated. This one miscalculation further created a drift in the calculation of important dates like that of the equinox and Easter. After over five centuries of efforts and attempts, this historic case of Cumulative Error was corrected and the Gregorian calendar came into application. By shortening the average year by 0.0075 days, the Gregorian calendar gave us our modern system of scheduling.

When compared to present-day accounts of Cumulative Error, the Julian calendar was a much better quandary—we were able to recognize and fix it. In our networked and overly connected lives, fake news and misinformation have become a norm. They continue to grow and remain unchecked. At their best, they create chaos, mistrust and fear-psychosis, and at their worst, they enable extremism, terrorism and violence.

The only way to prevent Cumulative Error is to learn from the experience of creating the Gregorian calendar. We must (a) Build capability to spot and identify error and misinformation; (b) Collate correct and accurate information; and (c) Be relentless in our pursuit of ensuring the original error is replaced from public memory.

SURVIVORSHIP BIAS

Never be judgemental or misunderstand people, things, concepts or events solely based on visible and obvious historical data. This may lead to false conclusions. Always think of the possible missing pieces of information and alternative perspectives.

Survivorship Bias or Survival Bias is the logical error of concentrating on people or things that made it past some selection process and overlooking those that did not, typically because of their lack of visibility. This can lead to false conclusions in several different ways.

During World War II, naval researchers concluded a study of damaged aircrafts that returned from missions. They used to analyse parts of the plane carefully and provide extra protection (armour) to the damaged parts in future missions. However, nothing changed. Things got worse, actually.

Hungarian mathematician Abraham Wald came to the rescue. His insight was simple—the researchers were only analysing planes that survived. What about those that didn't? His insight flipped the prevailing explanation on its head. He was able to prove that the areas with holes represented areas where a plane could be hit and still return safely. The parts of the plane without holes were the real danger. If hit there, planes did not return.

In the professional context, the merits of a formal college education are rightly debated on various forums. I understand why many experts think that even the best of educational institutions have basically become high premium insurance policies but discounting the merits of a formal college education by naming college dropouts like Mark Zuckerberg and Bill Gates is a glaring abuse of Survivorship Bias. It ignores the hundreds of thousands of dropouts who didn't accomplish anything. If we look at the entire spectrum of data of dropouts and their accomplishments, the picture isn't pretty. Basically, it is very hard to prove that going to college makes someone successful or dropping out of it propels achievement.

Survivorship Bias therefore paints a pretty, but an incomplete picture. It has a tendency to focus only on the visible evidence. By doing so it creates a polarized, unrealistic and inaccurate understanding of reality. To overcome Survivorship Bias, looking at the flip side, the missing data and forming a complete picture is important.

SIMPSON'S PARADOX

Trends and analyses that appear in small data-sets may disappear when amalgamated with a larger data-set. Do not assume data as a fact in itself. Always look at the variables and the data-set and beware of even the strongest correlations.

In the year 1973, University of California, Berkeley did a study on gender bias in graduate admissions for the university. According to the admissions data, it was clearly evident that men were favoured by the admissions committees. Men had a 45 per cent acceptance rate, while women had a 35 per cent acceptance rate. After looking at university level performance, the researcher next looked at individual departmental records. The results here were shocking. They showed that six out of eighty-five departments were significantly biased against men. On the other hand, only four departments were actually biased against women. The research then concluded that women tended to apply for more competitive departments. Whereas men applied for easier-to-get-into and less-competitive departments that relaxed their acceptance rates.

Named after Statistician Edward Simpson, the Simpson's Paradox is a popular social sciences and medical sciences phenomena in which there is a paradoxical relationship between the smaller data groups and the larger data-set.

In addition to highlighting the deviation in the data-set trends, Simpson's Paradox is an extremely relevant method to test the validity of trends, causal relations and parameters of a data-set. It is a mechanism to prevent exploitation or incorrect analysis of a limited data-set.

CONDORCET PARADOX

The Condorcet Paradox explores the cyclic nature of social choice even when the individual choice is transitive. That is, an individual might prefer candidate X to candidate Y, candidate Y to candidate Z and candidate Z to candidate X. Yet pick X or Z, and not Y. This is because conflicting majorities do not have an identify order of candidate preference.

In electoral or voting system where choices are non-binary the Condorcet Paradox appears. Instances where voters have more than two options to choose from, the electoral results are largely inconsistent and non-representative of individual preferences.

First noted by Marquis de Condorcet in the late 18th century, the Condorcet Paradox is a social choice theory. It states that despite having transitive individual choices, the social choice will be cyclic. The Condorcet Paradox is best explained with a thought experiment with three candidates A, B and C contesting elections, and three voters X, Y and Z voting. The experiment assumes that voter X's order of candidate preference is A, B and then C; for voter Y it is B, C and then A; and for voter Z it is C, A and B. In such a case, regardless of which candidate wins, two-third of the electorates' preference would not be accounted for.

Using the Condorcet Paradox, pollsters attempt to model actual election outcomes. This is done by extrapolating real data and modelling voting behaviour. Along with being a useful tool in predicting electoral results, the Condorcet Paradox is also a testament to the limitations of voting process. It has led to several voting reforms like two-stage voting process, enlarged electorates to limit the impact of the Condorcet Paradox, and cultural (and identity-based) impact on voting behaviours.

LIMITED HANGOUT

By self-exposing a previously hidden secret, politicians, journalists, etc., prevent a greater exposure of more detrimental information. It is a form of a propaganda technique.

In a very James Bond fashion, the term Limited Hangout originally gained currency as a spy-intelligence jargon during the American Watergate scandal in the 1970s. It is a popular deviation and distraction strategy. The act of deliberately revealing limited information to the public to divert them from a much more heinous, detrimental, scandalous or classified information.

It has three central implications. First, by voluntarily sharing true and useful information, a source may gain credibility which they can use later. It provides some immunity against counter-information in the future, and builds a positive reputation. Second, it desensitizes the public towards further scandalous and shocking information. It creates a new degree of morality and normalcy. Third, it protects the information that is 'hung out' from reaching public knowledge.

Limited Hangout has been an active tactic used not only by extremist groups and government intelligence agencies but also by some companies and businesses to maintain their reputation. Our modern systems of public affairs, media (online and offline) and information dissemination are a function of Limited Hangout.

FOCUSING ILLUSION

We see life, events, instances, people and concepts through different lenses and perspectives. By constantly focusing only on one lens or perspective, we distort opinions and create a biased understanding.

According to Nobel Laurette Daniel Kahneman, 'Nothing is ever as important as what you're thinking about while you're thinking about it.' This is something most of us have experienced. At some point or the other, we have all obsessed over a particular thing. By doing so, we magnify that particular thing so much in our head that it consumes and impacts all our thoughts. It becomes the prism from which we make sense of all other things.

Focusing Illusion is a key factor in determining the quality of our lives. It leads us to give excessive importance to one factor of our life and impairs our ability to gauge its future utility. For instance, attaching personal happiness to the need of buying material goods—a fancy new car, an expensive watch or possession of a rare artefact. Just like items, Focusing Illusion also works on intangible fixations. It could be an infatuation with a particular job, a dream school or invite to an exclusive event.

The best way to counter Focusing Illusion is to focus inward to identify what triggers it and then reach out to your trusted advisers to help you. It can be challenging to do this alone.

CHAPTER 60

ILLUSIONS AND BIASES

These set of mental models help us discover our own biases and judgement errors that arise when we see what we want to see and not the truth.

CONCEPT CREEP

As our empathy magnifies so does our reaction to issues of social oppression and violence. This may create an illusion of negative growth.

Concept Creep changes how we respond to social issues. For cognitive scientist Steven Pinker, decline in global violence altered our expectations and augmented human sensitivity.

With increased empathy, we became aware of micro-aggressions and subtle oppressions. However, on the flip side, it also increased the feeling of victimhood and diminished the agency of individuals and communities to overcome their own plight.

To positively optimize the Concept Creep, we must learn to distinguish facts from values (social constructions). Values and norms evolve with time. Both facts and values can change over time but it helps to know the difference.

STREETLIGHT EFFECT

Also known as the drunkard's research principle, it is the tendency to look for sources and information only in the easiest and most obvious places.

The story goes like this: There was a police officer who saw a drunk man under the streetlight trying to find something. On being asked, the drunk man answers that he dropped his key. The police officer offers to help him find it, and thereafter both of them, together, start searching under the streetlight. When, after a few minutes, they are unable to find it, the police officer enquires about the exact location at which the key was dropped. To this the drunk man exclaims—in the park. He is searching here, because this is where the light is.

A large chunk of social science research, historical understanding, scientific discoveries and popular perception is a function of the Streetlight Effect. We prioritize ease of access over our quest for truth.

Well-formulated research questions, objective enquiry and critical analysis are the best remedies for overcoming the Streetlight Effect.

BELIEF BIAS

Never approve an argument purely on basis of its conclusion. Always evaluate and judge an argument comprehensively. Critically analyse its propositions, assumptions, correlations, empirical support and deductions.

In most cases, it is difficult for us to look at all arguments and statements we hear with an objective lens. This is due to the sheer volume of information inflicted upon us. In most cases, our existing belief systems predetermine our reaction to any given statement.

Belief Bias is constantly at work in the way we consume news and information. We pick onto the headlines to form our opinions.

The more concurrent the conclusion is to our point of view, the more likely we are to believe it. This tendency thrives on three core factors—time, nature of content and culture of conformity. Therefore, to counter Belief Bias we can (a) Take more time and deliberation before reaching to conclusions; (b) Be critical of the way arguments and conclusions are given to us: Do they implicitly perpetuate a singular narrative? and (c) Question and resist the modern culture of conformity and the need for creating opinion-binaries.

PLURALISTIC IGNORANCE

Never blindly support a group decision simply because everyone around you seems to agree. Groups where people secretly disagree but collectively comply are inherently counterproductive. To avoid this, create a safe environment for conversation, expect people to disagree and actively listen for feedback.

Pluralistic Ignorance is a social collective bias that limits the ability of the individual to truly express themselves. It is a form of peer-pressure as well as group ignorance. Along with creating a toxic culture, Pluralistic Ignorance also leads to deleterious social consequences. A study by Kyushu University, Japan, shows the correlation between Pluralistic Ignorance and paternity leave. The research examined the attitudes and actions of Japanese male employees between the ages of 20 and 40 towards paternity leaves. Results showed that the men who had a positive outlook towards paternity leave were the ones who were avoiding taking it the most.

While the research does not include solutions to Pluralistic Ignorance, it does indicate the need for creating cultures conducive to authentic dialogue and limit the social fallouts of this collective bias.

THE PETRIE MULTIPLIER

Let's assume that there are six men and four women in a room. Each of the 10 individuals are equally likely to make rude, derogatory and sexist remarks. In this situation, women, by simply being lesser in number, will receive more negative comments. Therefore, even the smallest majority can be oppressive.

Conceptualized by computer scientist Karen Petrie, the Petrie Multiplier is a mathematical model or a thought experiment that studies the degree of negativity women receive. Popularly used in calculating sexism in the technology industry, the model claims that the extent of sexism women receive is the square of the gender ratio in that situation.

Just like sexism, the Petrie Multiplier can be applied to understand other forms of oppressions like racism, casteism, etc.

Building on this mathematical equality, we can further deduce that the easiest way to reduce oppression is to simply increase representation. This is something we robustly follow as we grow the Network Capital community. With over 100,000 members across 104 countries, the easiest and the most effective way for us to scale trust and create a safe and inclusive online space is to ensure diversity of individuals. By welcoming people from all ethnicities, nationalities, gender-orientations, cultural identities and regions, we are able to (a) Ensure representation; (b) Avoid echo-chambers; (c) Create safe and inclusive modern communities; and (d) Form meaningful connections.

WOOZLE EFFECT

Always be critical and thorough with the source of original information before building on it further. Integrity and reliability of information is always more important than the contents of the information.

The term 'woozle' comes from A. A. Milnes's *Winnie the Pooh*. It is based on Pooh and Pigglet's adventurous search of the 'woozle'—a rare and imaginary animal. It starts with Pigglet and Pooh coming across footprints left on the snow. They believe that the footprints belong to 'woozle' and decide to embark on a scavenger hunt to find the imaginary animal. As they proceed with their hunt, they create new footprints which they then follow. It is finally when Cristopher Robin intervenes that they realize that had been following their own footprints in circles.

Much of fake news and misinformation is a 'woozle'. Urban-myths and evidence-by-citation are important examples of the Woozle Effect. Like the footprints, pieces of information and research randomly appear in public discourse and on the internet. And before we realize, they snowball into complex webs of citations building upon one-another.

It is also important to note that unlike the unintentional footprints, the Woozle Effect is a deliberate and premeditated phenomenon in modern society and politics.

The Woozle Effect drastically increases the usage and responsibility of the fact and source checking mechanism. It also generates the need for personal diligence before believing and using any information.

TOCQUEVILLE PARADOX

Modern discontent with social conditions is a product of the exponential increase in our expectations compared to our realities. This gap between expectations and realities breeds frustration.

2019 was a year of global turmoil and unrest. As massive protests and uprisings rocked Hong Kong, New Delhi, Sudan, Lebanon, Iran, and Iraq, other countries like the United Kingdom, Chile, United States, etc., witnessed small and sporadic unrests. In all these regions, there wasn't a singular cause of discontent. However, the meta-themes included calls for increased autonomy, resistance against authoritarianism and the urgency for change.

If, as an experiment, we were to study past conditions of quality of individual life with present standards of living in each of these countries, we will see a clear pattern of drastic improvement. India in the last century has progressed for a colonial dependant state to a thriving economy and sovereign country. Life expectancy has increased from the age of 41 years in the year 1960 to 68 years in the year 2020. Literacy rate has gone up to 74 per cent. GDP per capita has gone from USD 753 in the year 1960 to USD 1670 in the year 2016. The country has been successful in legally abolishing major practices of discrimination, homophobic laws and gendered distribution of property. Yet large populations of India (like the other countries) are still discontent.

French political scientist, Alexis de Tocqueville first defined the Tocqueville Paradox in the year 1840. He wrote that as democracy, privilege and standards of living increase, our expectations from the society will catapult. This will create a gap between expectations and realities that will cultivate discontent.

With increased access to information, heightened realization of disparity and social media, the Tocqueville Paradox has become the toxic reality of our collective society. At the individual level it has created choice-paralysis, that is, our inability to choose due to multiplicity of options. The difficulty in deciding which movie to watch from across the different streaming platforms is a typical example.

Despite is limitations, the Tocqueville Paradox is an important tool in expanding and retaining our hard-earned freedom.

ULTIMATE ATTRIBUTION ERROR

People have the tendency to attribute positive acts by known individuals to their character and negative acts to their situation, while doing the reverse for their adversaries.

A study conducted in the year 1976 by B. L. Duncan, found that 'white' students were more likely to interpret a shove as violent and more likely to explain it disproportionately when the shove came from a 'black' person as opposed to a 'white' person. Other similar Ultimate Attribution Errors plague our lives.

We do not understand acts and events in their unique context. Instead, we embed them in our larger biased understanding and relationships with the individuals associated with the act. By doing so, we arbitrarily associate positive acts to our allies, and negative situations to our opponents. Therefore, Ultimate Attribution Error leads to cognitive failure on two levels. First, we are unable to clearly and objectively understand the given event, and second, it strengthens and reinforces biases.

Just like in the case of individuals, Ultimate Attribution Error also functions at group levels. It attributes negative out-group prejudice and stereotyping—cunning Jews, conservative Christians and violent Muslims.

To avoid the Ultimate Attribution Errors, think beyond the individual or the group and look at the situation objectively. It will not only give you a much clearer understanding of the event but also give you opportunities for forging new relationships and abandoning redundant lies.

GOLDEN HAMMER

For an individual with a hammer, everything is a nail. People with niche area specific knowledge, or unique expertise have a propensity of looking at all issues with that one idea that they are proficient in.

There is a popular phrase, 'For someone with a hammer, everything is a nail.' This one sentence is the core essence of the Golden Hammer principle. As we academically or professionally specialize in a particular skill or area, we increasingly tend to apply that skill to all aspects of our understanding. We thereby loose our ability to look at an issue from a different perspective.

For a cardiologist, most medical ailments lead to the heart. For a python expert, all data analysis is python. For an African studies researcher, all issues are about race and geography. Therefore, at the individual level, the Golden Hammer leads to a lopsided and limited understanding of different events. At the group level is perpetuates complacency and decreases creativity.

According to the World Economic Forum *2019 Future of Work* report, the decade will see a rise in appreciation of inter-sectoral and inter-disciplinary work. The Golden Hammer will then become a major barrier to professional growth. To mitigate the negative impact, we should (a) constantly work to learn new and changing skills and (b) work at the inter-sections of things.

CHAPTER 61

MAXIMS AND CAUTIONARY TALES

Here we explore and flip common maxims and operating principles to avoid costly mistakes.

PARETO PRINCIPLE

Eighty per cent of results come from 20 per cent of actions.

Italian economist Vilfredo Pareto in the year 1895 observed that there was natural division in the society between the 'vital few' (the top 20 per cent) and the 'trivial many' (the bottom 80 per cent). However, more than being a useful way of understanding the society, the Pareto Principle became a critical tool of application.

Most start-ups as well as companies follow the Pareto Principle in determining their tasks. They recognize that 80 per cent of their work will happen in just 20 per cent of the time. But the remaining 20 per cent of the assignments will take 80 per cent of the effort. This recognition helps them not only plan their work but also prioritize their tasks. It is a core principle applicable to most of projects. Just like in business, the Pareto Principle finds relevant applications in the domain of economics, computing, sports, mathematics, etc.

At a personal level the Pareto Principle is a useful tool in arranging and budgeting our time to our different interests, hobbies, work assignments and social engagements. Every time you plan your calendar, think of the Pareto Principle, that is, think of maximizing 80 per cent benefits by spending 20 per cent of your time. Also account for the un-skippable 20 per cent of the tasks that require 80 per cent of your attention.

NIRVANA FALLACY

It is a natural impulse to compare actual events, practices or solutions to utopian ideals. However, by doing so we not only create a false dichotomy but also reduce the space for constructive actions.

French Philosopher, Voltaire, while exploring the human need for perfection proclaimed, 'Perfect is the enemy of good.' The Nirvana Fallacy is quite similar to Voltaire's writings. It is our tendency to reject and disapprove certain actions or events because they do not match up to our perfect and utopian ideals.

Entrepreneurs very often face Nirvana Fallacy before putting their product in the market. They tend to set unrealistic goals and timelines for the product, and are not ready to compromise on them. At best this leads to some delays in the product launch, and at worse it leads to a situation in which the product is never launched. To counter the Nirvana Fallacy, LinkedIn founder, Reid Hoffman famously said, 'If you're not embarrassed of the first version of your product, you launched it too late.'

Just like start-ups, Nirvana Fallacy dictates our personal goals and ambitions. It creates a perception of a dichotomy between an ideal situation and improbable action, and an unfavourable situation and realistic action. Just as Voltaire pointed it out, we must choose the unfavourable yet realistic action. The quest for the ideal and unattainable will leave us crippled and worse-off.

EMOTIVE CONJUGATION

Most words, phrases and sentences are a combination of factual and emotional content. To accurately distil the message, it is important to distinguish between the factual and emotional content.

Emotive Conjugation is a combination of rhetorical, psychological and linguistics factors that alter and form our opinions. Contrary to popular understanding, facts have a very minimal role to play. Therefore, we can actually completely change our opinion of people without actually changing the facts. Emotive Conjugation is built on the foundational principle that our mind constantly looks beyond what is true while forming opinions. It instead looks at the social consequences of having a particular opinion. This enables our tendency to mirror the emotions and opinions of the source of our information.

With traditional and accountable sources of information being replaced by decentralized and anonymous sources, we have entered an era of opinion overload. To successfully navigate in this time, it is more important than ever to build and retain empathy and to listen to a spectrum of opinions on one issue without getting agitated.

ENANTIODROMIA

It is the propensity of things to turn into their complete opposites. This happens typically when too much of one thing leads to the rise of its own antithesis.

Introduced by Swiss psychiatrist, Carl Jung, Enantiodromia is the process of emergence of unconscious opposites over the course of time. In an almost karmic manner, Enantiodromia is simply too much of one thing leading to emergence of its own opposite.

The modern celebrations of workplace positivity are a case in point. In the 2010s, with bright walls, cheerful quotes and an obligatory upbeat attitude, a new work culture emerged. As start-ups and coworking spaces grew beyond limited hubs like the Silicon Valley this culture expanded across the world. Overtime it intensified so much that today it has been overcome with a toxic culture of forced happiness. What started as an attempt to improve mental health and optimism at the work place has now become a cause for stress. Such toxic positivity helps no one and is a useful example of enantiodromia.

HALO EFFECT

It is a cognitive bias that leads people to take one positive trait or characteristic as applicable in other areas as well.

The idea, 'First impressions are the last impressions' is the hallmark of Halo Effect. It was first developed by a psychologist Edward Thorndike in the year 1920. It was part of Thorndike's research that attempted to study how one positive or negative characteristic would drag an individual's understanding of all other traits. The research concluded that the effect works both positively and negatively.

Today, researchers have shown that the Halo Effect is not just limited to individuals. Halo Effect is also applicable to businesses, websites, products, organizations, etc. An example of the Halo Effect in businesses would be through celebrity brand endorsements and creating iconic advertisements. For websites and online platforms, it might be a feature that we like or the aesthetics of the website. In case of individuals, it might be based on inter-personal relations or particular characteristics.

To avoid falling prey to the Halo Effect, it is important to build our capabilities of identifying cases of Halo Effect. We can do this by (a) being thoughtful in building our initial perception; (b) recognizing why we prioritize certain characteristics, features or endorsements over others; and (c) always considering the alternative.

OUT-GROUP HOMOGENEITY EFFECT

Each individual is product of multiple interests, identities and beliefs. Never stereotype or categorize people based on just one of these aspects.

Till the 17th century, individual human identity was largely interchangeable with community (group) identity. This was due to the fact that the idea of an individual self was unknown, and membership to communities was restricted. Each human was a part one community or tribe which defined their identity. This helped one community understand the other community, and build ties and relationships based on the understanding.

As ideas of liberty, individualism and freedom grew, group dynamics changed. The original celebration of homogeneous groups was replaced by the celebration of diversity within groups. Instead of focusing on the shared commonality, groups now cherish the uniqueness of its members. Therefore, in the last three centuries we have seen a compete change in in-group dynamics. Yet out-group understandings remain the same, that is, we still see other groups as homogenous entities. This is what social psychologists call the 'Out-group Homogeneity Effect'.

Out-group Homogeneity Effect is now a popular form of cognitive bias. In our globalized modern society, human interests and identities are dynamic. They change across time and space. Therefore, the historically productive practice of stereotyping and ascribing group identities to individuals is now redundant. Rather modern groups are extremely complex and conflicting. Stereotyping leads to a defunct understanding of social relations and group dynamics.

MATTHEW PRINCIPLE

It is a theory of accumulation. According to the Matthew Principle, advantages as well as disadvantages get concentrated overtime. This makes it easier for the rich to get richer, the poor to get poorer and the smart to get smarter.

As young children, most of us are told to read books. This advice is built on the premise that it is easier to build habits when young. The more you read as a child, the easier reading gets in general. In case of reading, the Matthew Principle works at two levels. First, it makes the practice of reading easy and fun. Second, it leads to aggregation of knowledge which makes understanding new concepts and ideas easier.

This term was coined by Robert K. Merton to describe how popular and well-known scientists tend to receive more attention and acclaim simply by the virtue of already being acclaimed, while scientists with lesser recognition, yet similar work, struggle to get acclaim.

At the collective level the Matthew Principle has crucial implications for our society. It shows how certain countries do well, because they have historically done well. Or how certain privileged sections of the society continue to accumulate wealth and entitlements, while the disadvantaged sections face newer forms of oppression. The only way to flip the Matthew Principle socially is to create new individual level advantages by building personal habits and practises that go on to disrupt societal trends. Social upward mobility through education is an important case in point.

PETER PRINCIPLE

Workplace hierarchies enable growth of individuals only till they reach their highest point of incompetence, that is, people rise in their workplace till the time they succeed in their previous role. This system either leads to getting fired or incompetence and work stagnation.

Businesses, governments and organizations perpetuate a very linear idea of hierarchy, promotion and growth. They create a straightforward path of progression based on time, competency and authority.

The Peter Principle thrived in the world that was trying to build capacities of mass-production, centralized and hierarchical administration and standardized work-systems. The success of Fordism and 20th-century capitalism is largely due to Peter Principle. However, despite its 20th-century success, it is becoming irrelevant in the 21st century. In contemporary workplaces, the Peter

Principle is emerging as a barrier to creativity and innovation and as a result, a barrier to economic progress.

As the imperative mode of economic production shifts from material goods to unique services, the Peter Principle increasingly becomes unfavourable. The idea of promotion, a crucial aspect of the Peter Principle, has drastically changed in organizations. Unlike before, for a salesperson or coder to become a manager, is no more an obvious progression. Rather, it might even be counterproductive for them.

While there is general recognition that the Peter Principle is counterproductive, it is in vogue and shows up in subtle ways.

LOKI'S WAGER

We, at times, defend a concept from criticism by reducing it to either a myth, or an undefinable phenomenon. This reduction involves use of vague justifications like 'some things are just meant to be', etc.

Legend has it, Loki from the Marvel universe made a bet with some dwarves and lost. He had to pay in the form of his head. To escape he created massive confusion, ambiguity and contradiction by adding a clause to the bet. The clause entailed that no part of his neck could be taken while cutting the head. As dwarves could not reach a consensus on where the neck ends and the head starts, Loki escaped his payment.

Loki's wager suggests that if there is enough ambiguity, contradiction and confusion any outcome is possible. It is a classic tactic employed by some politicians and prime time news anchors. We also observe Loki's wager in full swing on politically charged social media groups.

The best way to avoid or transform a Loki's Wager like situation, is to (a) Identify the aim and context of the concept and conversation; (b) Understand where the other side is coming from; (c) Be careful with your words and language; and (d) Learn to agree to disagree and step-back from conversations.

SUB-SELVES

All of us are a sum of our different mental processes. We have multiple sub-selves that cohesively and simultaneously function within us. Different situations and contexts bring our different sub-selves to the forefront.

While the concept of sub-selves comes in the domain of cognitive science and psychology, study of literature and fiction is probably the best way of understanding sub-selves. Authors like Shakespeare, Sylvia Plath, Amrita Pritam, etc., in their writings explore the nuances of the conflicting selves. They build complex and real characters who provide us with insights to the sub-selves. Literature beautifully explores the roles of the different sub-selves, along with providing a glimpse into how the multiple selves interact and inform one another.

Typically, sub-selves are a combination of our genetics, environment, experiences, context and emotions. Therefore, there is not one 'true-self'. Rather, each of our traits and characteristics, like being funny, lazy, ambitious, etc., are just a part of one of our sub-selves. Understanding the different mental processes and the multiple characteristics that define 'you', is extremely important to unpack our actions, intents and capabilities. Proust's writing sums up the idea of sub-selves as 'the several gentlemen, of whom I consist'.

Our sub-self does not form a singular personality. Instead, our sub-selves enable a 'network of personalities'. Reflection and meditation are the most effective tools to make sense of this network.

CHAPTER 62

PRECISION OF THOUGHTS, COMMON PITFALLS

Clarity is power. Like everything else, it is an acquired skill that comes from training our thoughts to follow a structured rhythm.

GOODHART'S LAW

Never let the goal be conceptualized purely in numeric terms. It is not only reductionist, but it may also lead to unintended consequences. For example, to control and remove snakes in India, the British colonialists started offering money for snake skins. In response to this, Indian natives started breeding snakes and then killing them for the money.

According to British Anthropologist, Marilyn Strathern, 'When a measure becomes a goal, it ceases to become a measure.' By reducing a goal to a mere quantity, we drastically alter its quality. In extreme cases, we also alter the outcome.

Through the different stages of building the Network Capital community, we set multiple goals for ourselves. These goals have always been formulated in a way that bridged the gap between our long-term aspirations and short-terms plans. And till date, we have never adopted simplistic numeric targets. Our goals have typically been formulated by quantifying the quality of our progress. Our target, therefore, is not to reach a given number of new members per month. Instead, we measure progress in terms of the meaningful connections we enable, or the instances in which we add value to someone's experience. This method of setting goals and tracking progress has helped Network Capital grow in a sustainable yet scalable manner.

The best way to counter the Goodhart's law is to always be conscious of the consequences setting a particular target. Along with consequences, it is also important to set proper metrics of tracking the progression. Our goals need to be designed and conceptualized in such a way that they lead to real progress.

RADICAL PHASE TRANSITION

Extremist movements move from solids (tyrannies), to liquids (insurgencies) and gases (conspiracy theories). Pressuring them reverses their progression. It causes them to go from solid, to liquid, to gas. Leaving them alone enables them to move from gas, to liquid, to solid.

Historians and academicians associate the British policy of indifference and ignorance as one of the key factors that enabled the rise of Hitler and Nazis in Germany. Popularly known as the policy of 'appeasement', the British government believed that after the 1919 Treaty of Versailles, Germany had genuine grievances. The Prime Minister Chamberlin expected that if Hitler was left alone, he would become less demanding and radical.

Between the years 1919 and 1938, the policy of appeasement gave space for the Nazi ideology to grow and thrive. However, as Hitler gained immense power and control, Chamberlin was ousted from power in United Kingdom. What follows next is the most violent war of human history, the World War II.

Radical and extremist groups that are growing today follow the same logic. While they might not have the same potential in terms of violence and war, our inaction towards them is giving space for these fringe groups to transition from conspiracy theories to insurgencies and eventually tyrannies. To proactively counter their rise, we need to take decisive actions and counter-measures to defuse their growth.

LEGIBILITY

In the process of transforming 'messy' natural systems into 'legible' and codified processes, we tend to miss essential components of that system. This causes inherent failures and contradictions in the new legible process.

Historically human curiosity has led to multi endeavours that attempted to decode natural systems and processes. It has informed our understanding of subjects like philosophy, mathematics, physics, etc. As our ability to understand natural systems grew, our interest in converting these 'messy' natural systems into 'legible' codified processes increased.

Today, legibility in one of the most crucial barriers in digitalization of any existing social process or natural system. For instance, social media platforms are essentially attempts to create neat systems and mechanisms of social interaction. Therefore, different social media platforms enable different forms and types of communication. Twitter makes us think quicker and formulate to the point ideas, Instagram makes us interact visually and Facebook is a combination of our status updates and information influx.

The digitalization of social interactions and interpersonal relations has created streamlined channels and formats of exchange. Determined by digital architectures, networks and algorithms, our online social interaction can be represented in the form of data and equation. However, by replacing our 'messy' system of social interaction, essential components that regulated communication have been missed. Instead, we have created echo-chambers of our own thoughts and scaled misinformation. Culture specific components of dialogue, debate and deliberations have not made their way online. Therefore, as we continue to take other natural systems like social interactions and transform them into legible structures, we need to be cognizant of the 'messy' pieces we ignore or leave behind.

SHIFTING BASELINE SYNDROME

We tend to become oblivious to things that we are familiar with and as the world is always changing, our conception of 'normal' is also constantly getting updated. In extreme cases, we are becoming blind to our own slow march towards catastrophe.

The Shifting Baseline Syndrome comes from fisheries scientist, Daniel Pauly's, research from the 1990s. Pauly observed that his fellow researchers would compare a given fish stock to a baseline set at the start of their respective careers. Therefore, each individual researcher had a completely different definition of the 'normal' or baseline fish stock. A similar pattern of inconsistent and changing baselines can also be observed in other situations.

For instance, our notions of 'normal' level of greenery and the appropriate number of trees and vegetation have been constantly changing. So has our understanding of climate change, weather patterns and temperature. For the residents of New Delhi in the year 2020, a temperature of 45° Celsius in summers is normal, while for residents of New Delhi in the year 1980, a temperature of 35° C was typical. Therefore, by taking general information and things as a given, we ignore historical developments. We continuously become accustomed to new ideas of 'normal' and neglect systemic changes.

We also need to be cognizant of the fact that the Shifting Baseline Syndrome functions both at the personal level, as well as, at the generational level. Therefore, data is probably our best bet against the Shifting Baseline Syndrome. By taking stock of progression and change on the basis verified data, we would be better prepared to navigate systemic changes and prevent catastrophes.

AVAILABILITY CASCADE

Availability Cascade is a self-enforcing process in which a new idea or concept gains currency simply by the virtue of being new. People may agree or disagree, either way, their reaction to the concept invariably amplifies it.

The idea of Availability Cascade was first developed by Timur Kuran and Cass Sunstein.

The #MeToo movement in 2017 came like a tsunami. In a short span of time it went from being an American discussion on sexual-abuse allegations against Harvey Weinstein to a global discourse on gender-based violence. Most, if not all, internet using audience engaged with the #MeToo movement. The movement made us all aware, it forced most of us to think and led many of us to react. This awareness, thought and action created a reinforcing cycle of growth that emerged as a pivotal contributor to the scale of the #MeToo movement. Today, the #MeToo movement has led to tangible legislative changes and judicial convictions.

In theoretical terms, the #MeToo movement is an important example of the availability cascade effect. Typically, Availability Cascade is a composite process that involves the following.

1. *Informational cascade:* Self-enforcing process of information transmission. It creates a situation where people base their stance and opinion on information provided by others, assuming that others are more knowledgeable.
2. *Reputational cascade:* To avoid social disapproval and criticism, people tend to spread and support certain opinions and perspectives online, while they actually may not believe in the said opinion.

Information and reputational cascade together facilitate the Availability Cascade. Building on this concept, Nobel Laurette, Daniel Kahneman, in his book *Thinking, Fast and Slow* develops the idea of availability entrepreneurs. Availability entrepreneurs are individuals and organizations that leverage availability cascade to further a certain goal or agenda.

REACTANCE THEORY

Imposing restrictions on behaviour, action or expression rarely achieve their desired goal. Instead of changing or replacing the original position, the restrictions strengthen it.

One of the most banal plotlines of cartoons is a scene in which a character presses the huge-red-button which reads 'do not press', solely because it says 'do not press'. Very simply put, Reactance Theory is much like that cartoon scene; it plays on our impulse to resist restrictions.

Coined in the year 1966 by American psychologist, Jack Brehm, the Reactance Theory explores human reaction to freedom and restrictions. According to Professor Brehm, Reactance Theory has two guiding principles. First, the magnitude of perceived freedom is directly proportional to the reaction on its removal. In other words, the more importance and value we ascribe to the perceived freedom, the more we would resist and react to restrictions. Second, in cases where more than one freedom is threatened at the same time, the reaction and resistance also multiply.

Periods of mass censorship are quintessential examples of Reactance Theory. For instance, the Vernacular Press Act, 1878, imposed by the British Rule in India, fuelled growth of rebel songs, stories, pamphlets and posters. These rebel publications not only escaped censorship by twisting the law, they also increased the efforts of rebels in producing and spreading these publications.

Reactance Theory is, therefore, an important aspect of 'reverse psychology'. An understanding of this theory is vital in scenarios where we attempt to create common cultures, behaviours and practices. Based on the Reactance Theory and the experience of building the Network Capital community, restrictions never work.

Instead, the practice of featuring positive practices and nudging towards a collaborative and corrective behaviour, works better in building progressive cultures.

PREDICTIVE CODING

Predictive Coding is our cognitive ability to organize thoughts and experiences as efficiently as possible. It is our minds' system of processing general environment and data. It replaces the unknown with the expected.

We encounter numerous objects, experiences and individuals daily. On most typical days we all see at least one tree, some preparation of food and some form of human interaction. The fact that these observations and experiences are so trivial that they do not fascinate us is a result of Predictive Coding. All of our imagination, mental visualizations and thought processing is a part of Predictive Coding. Therefore, at a meta level, responding to input is the by-product. The act of receiving and processing input is foundational to the functioning of our brain.

Predictive Coding is undoubtingly essential for our brains' ability to receive, process and respond to inputs from our environment. As a mechanism, it limits the stimuli to our brain by putting new and unknown objects and experiences in existing categories of known. By doing so, Predictive Coding exponentially increases our abilities of concentration and dealing with changing environments. It saves us from obsessively thinking or being fascinated by every new tree, food item and individual we meet. Imagine being distraught and fascinated by every meal you eat. Without Predictive Coding we would never be able to work on second-order thinking and complex problems.

Predictive Coding also has a critical impact on our learning and memory. However, in this case it creates an interesting Catch-22. To learn and unlearn new information and knowledge, our minds have to work against our natural predictive coding processes. But to remember all that we have learnt, we need to generate and strengthen a predictive model of that information. Optimal success in this case lies at delicate balance between learning and memory. It also makes it extremely important for us to be careful, conscious and deliberate in things we attempt to learn and unlearn. For example, understanding mental models and forms of cognitive biases would be a point in favour of learning.

APOPHENIA

We have a limited ability to comprehend data. Therefore, to make sense of the abstraction, we impose our imagination on arrangements of data. We create patterns where none exist.

A ball, bat and pitch in themselves mean nothing. Human minds have the unique ability to draw patterns, dots and connections from seemingly unrelated pieces of information. The patterns we draw are informed by our personal biases and narratives. Therefore, based on our personal context, that ball, bat and pitch could mean the sport of cricket, baseball, both or something completely different.

Much of the conspiracy theories as well as pieces of creativity are a product of Apophenia. The process typically involves an individual (or a group of individuals) piecing together random articles of observation, news and information to create convincing narratives. Even study of data and census is influenced by Apophenia. In many cases, it subconsciously determines the variables, sample audience and research parameters. It handicaps our ability to objectively analyse. Building on this core theme, Nobel Laureate Robert Schiller has written extensively on what he calls 'narrative economics'. Narrative economics is 'the study of the spread and dynamics of popular narratives, the stories, particularly those of human interest and emotions, and how these change through time, to understand economic fluctuations'.

Schiller's scholarship on narrative economics is a critical tool in countervailing Apophenia in a constructive manner. By building and leveraging an acute understanding of patterns we can unpack modern developments.

NARRATIVE FALLACY

We tend to see facts and interpret them as stories. We thread facts together to form a hypothetical chain of cause and effect. This hypothesis in most cases is based on our subjective experiences and reality.

While we would all like to believe that we are objective and rational beings, in most instances we are not. We have a tendency to visualize facts as part of stories we are familiar with.

Nassim Taleb in his book *The Black Swan* popularized the term 'Narrative Fallacy'. He eloquently argued that humans seek explanations to the point of manufacturing. Scholar Michael Shermer calls this habit of seeing meaningful patterns in meaningless things as 'Patternicity'. In its extreme form, Narrative Fallacy inspires regressive ritualistic traditions. And in its moderate form, it enables reductionist, short-sighted and obscure decision-making.

For Warren Buffet, the best way to resist the Narrative Fallacy is to build our ability to argue the opposing sides of any narrative that you support.

PAREIDOLIA

For most of human history, predators stalked the planet. Survival of the fittest was a reality in its literal sense. In such a context, survival invariably favoured the paranoid. It favoured people paranoid enough to see the malevolent even in a shadow. While this paranoia served as an essential defence mechanism, it has now cursed us with Pareidolia or the tendency to see faces in things.

We all see faces in different (at times weird) things. Sometimes it is a car with its headlights that resembles the human face or a funny looking potato or maybe a non-descript dustbin. For Diane Duyser, it was a face of women in her cheese toast. While at first it scared her, but the soft features of the female face on her toast also fascinated Diane. As the word about the cheese toast got around, it eventually became so popular that a casino paid $28,000 to display it.

This tendency to see faces in inanimate objects is not new. According to researchers, it is partly due to how human brains are wired, partly due to the sheer number of faces we see, and partly a product of paranoia and evolutionary processes. Facial expressions have always been a crucial way to gauge emotions and motives. They humanize our understanding of objects and inform our subconscious reaction. Psychologists have built experiments and tests based on Pareidolia to examine personal characteristics and emotional functioning. The Rorschach inkblot test is an interesting and popular example. This test presents individuals with slides of inkblots and checks their emotional health and traits based on their perception of the abstract inkblots.

Pareidolia is therefore an extremely crucial form of non-verbal communication and awareness. But the fear and paranoia associated with Pareidolia are now irrelevant. As was with Diane, the experience of seeing faces in things like bread can instinctively be scary. Historically, the odds of being scared and paranoid worked in our favour. It saved us from all sorts of harms and attacks. However, with modern societies, collective living and improved standard of life, paranoia and fear are counterproductive. Even Naval Ravikant, AngelList's CEO claims it is better to be an irrational optimist than a cynical pessimist. Therefore, to make Pareidolia work in your favour, embrace its abilities of humanizing, communication and perception and resist its capabilities of instilling fear and paranoia.

INVERSE THINKING: FLIPPING A PROBLEM UPSIDE DOWN MAKES IT SOLVABLE

Inverting a problem to find solutions is a concept I heard from Charlie Munger. Inspired by the mathematician Carl Jacobi, he said:

Invert, always invert: Turn a situation or problem upside down. Look at it backward. What happens if all our plans go wrong? Where don't we want to go, and how do you get there? Instead of looking for success, make a list of how to fail instead—through sloth, envy, resentment, self-pity, entitlement, all the mental habits of self-defeat. Avoid these qualities and you will succeed. Tell me where I'm going to die, that is, so I don't go there.

Warren Buffett has a similar take:

'Charlie and I have not learned how to solve difficult business problems. What we have learned is to avoid them.'

Instead of asking ourselves what will help us create a great career, we need to root out factors that will surely lead to an unfulfilling career. Failure is a far better teacher than success can ever be. We need to start by identifying and reflecting upon times we failed. As Mark Twain so meaningfully said, 'History doesn't repeat itself but it often rhymes.' This holds true for our mistakes as well. We tend to repeat the same mistakes over and over again. Life does not give us the opportunity to make everyone's mistakes so we must learn from our mistakes and that of our peers.

One of the biggest mistakes students and young professionals make is to network insanely without hearing their own voice. The result is that they end up applying for all kinds of jobs and simultaneously pursuing multiple pathways. In their head, they are increasing their optionality but in essence, they are deluding themselves. Year after year, the pattern repeats itself.

Just to counter that, we set up a failure lab on Network Capital. It is a compendium where our community members anonymously share their failures and reflect on what they learned from it. The list is accessible to all our community members and helps them learn from mistakes of their peers.

While some people might think that we are being overly cautious by focusing on mistakes, I feel that being aware of identifiable, avoidable risks empowers us. Of course, some of us could become paranoid and obsess over trivial things but with practice we can learn to get to the root of the matter efficiently. Like most things in life, it is an acquired skill.

CHAPTER 63

THINKING THOROUGHLY

We often think and listen to our whims and biases. To explore the truth, we need to understand our triggers with intention and purpose.

ACTIVE LISTENING: LISTENING WITHOUT JUMPING TO SPEAK NEXT

This mental model can be summed up as being a sponge and a filter. It is much harder than it sounds. In most circumstances, people are waiting to respond based on what they thought you said. Instead of focusing on your context or your actual words, their energy is focused on figuring out a response that makes them look smart. It is not just them; you do the same.

In the off chance that you actually heard what the other person said, you go back to your standard repertoire of words. Remember the last time the waiter at the restaurant asked you how your meal was? What did you say; most likely that 'it was great'. Remember the last time someone asked you how you were? What did you say? Most likely—'doing well/great'.

There is a reason why we overuse/abuse the word 'awesome'. Everything isn't and shouldn't be awesome.

However, this mental model isn't about language. I am invoking language so that you can evaluate how you listen and what you listen to. If you are like most of us, you listen to what you want to listen to. When it comes to views on stocks or politics, you automatically filter out stuff you don't believe in.

It limits both your world view and your learning. Even when you fundamentally disagree with someone and wish to argue with them/prove them wrong (although proving someone wrong usually doesn't accomplish anything), you need to know where they are coming from and understand why they are saying what they are saying. In other words, be a sponge.

A sponge absorbs everything but if you absorb everything, you become clunky and confused. You need to train yourself to filter out stuff that is not rooted in real experience, philosophy, data and experiments.

Building solid ways of thinking needs mental models and they emerge from the process of first absorbing, then analysing and finally weeding out stuff that doesn't add up.

Try and do three things this week.

First, don't ask anyone 'how are you'. Replace this with something else, something slightly less generic.

Second, when someone asks you how things are, don't instantly respond 'great' or 'awesome'. Reflect for a moment and express what you are actually up to.

Third, have coffee with someone you know does not share your views.

Time to train your active listening muscles!

INSTANT GRATIFICATION: 'UBER' FOR SHORT-TERM PLEASURE

Instant Gratification is the desire to experience pleasure or fulfilment without delay or deferment. Think of it as 'Uber' for pleasure. As weird as it sounds, most of us end up prioritizing instant gratification over long-term happiness and satisfaction. There is nothing new about it.

Our mind paraphrases what John Maynard Keynes said about long-term consequences—'In the long run, we are all dead', and then adds English philosopher Thomas Hobbes' less than optimistic commentary on our lives—'And the life of man— solitary, poor, nasty, brutish, and short'.

So, if life is nasty, brutish and short, and we are all dead in the long run, it makes sense to live in the moment and for it. However, much has changed since the time of Moore in terms of life expectancy, communities, expectations, etc. Surprisingly, our insatiable quest for instant pleasure remains the same. In fact, with the mainstreaming of the gig economy, it now has powerful wings.

Instant Gratification is a mental model simply because knowing how we are wired can help us watch out for times when we are dancing to the whims of our monkey mind. It matters because it hinders good decision-making.

FIRST-PRINCIPLES THINKING

First Principles are a group of self-evident assumptions that cannot be reduced any further. Think of our knowledge as a collection of Lego blocks. The most robust Lego structures are the ones with solid foundations. If the emerging structure wobbles, it will eventually break with the slightest of disturbances. Similarly, if the foundation of what we know is built upon misplaced conventions and hearsay, it is safe to say that we don't know very much.

Unfortunately, most of our schools and colleges pay very little emphasis on the foundation and a disproportionate emphasis on the façade. We aren't encouraged to question the commonly held and often misplaced conventions. Instead we are incentivized to accept norms and follow the beaten path. The result is that our internal operating system gets corrupted and our decision-making faculties are significantly reduced.

Knowledge is combinatorial which means that the true power is unleashed when we bring together seemingly disparate thoughts together. *Apple* worked because it combined fashion and technology. It was a better tech company than any fashion company and a better fashion company than any tech company at the same time.

Almost all great innovators, writers and thinkers have one thing in common—they think from First Principles. That is why they are able to juxtapose different strands of knowledge and create something original, something meaningful. Leonardo Da Vinci combined the best of arts and engineering to create something the world craved but had never seen.

We can't expect to build *Apple* or be like Leonardo Da Vinci in a day, but by learning from what worked for them, we can get slightly better each day, truly unleashing the power of compounding over time.

OCKHAM'S RAZOR

Named after the 14th century English philosopher William of Ockham, this guiding principle states that the simplest explanation is most likely to be true.

When we have two competing explanations, we should start with the simplest one. Complications are usually man-made. The reason we call it Ockham's Razor is that it shaves off needless assumptions and knowledge that is derived from conventional norms. Those who don't think from first principles should surely give Ockham's Razor a shot. It is important to keep in mind that this is not a law, just a mental model we should keep in mind. A helpful quote by Einstein explains it well—'Everything should be made as simple as possible, but no simpler.' While many Einstein quotes were not uttered by him, this one has been verified, thanks to Roger Sessions from his article published in the New York Times in the year 1950.

HANLON'S RAZOR

Never attribute to malice what can be explained by carelessness or stupidity. In simple words, give people the benefit of doubt.

By virtue of running a large yet intimate global community, I get thousands of messages and emails every day. While I try to respond to as many as possible, I always fall short. Sometimes I send short, cryptic messages and sometimes I just declare email bankruptcy which means that I archive all emails up till a certain time and start afresh. In this process, I end up unintentionally rubbing people the wrong way, especially those who have not seen Network Capital from its initial stages.

Someone who has taken the effort to reach out to me rightly expects to get a reply. It is impossible for him to take a look at my inbox. S/he subconsciously attributes my actions to malice even though that is not the case—far from it.

That's why it is important to keep Hanlon's Razor in mind in today's perennially connected society where we text more than we meet, date people living in different time zones and are constantly bombarded with cute quotes on productivity.

However, there is a catch. If you are having to give someone the benefit of doubt every day, it is advisable to explore the dynamics of the relationship in greater detail. You don't want to impose upon someone or be ignored by someone. Your time is as precious as theirs.

If you are not a priority for them despite trying to reach them through all possible ways (email, text, voice message, phone—in that order), it is time for a graceful exit. However, there is still no need to hold a grudge.

CONJUNCTION FALLACY

Most of us are hardwired to over-analyse and relate assumptions that aren't true.

Conjunction Fallacy has been studied at length by Amos Tversky and Nobel Laureate Daniel Kahneman. They provided various examples of Conjunction Fallacy in the October 1983 edition of Psychology Review.

The most oft-cited example of this fallacy is as follows:

Linda is 31 years old, single, outspoken and very bright. She majored in philosophy. As a student, she was deeply concerned with issues of discrimination and social justice, and also participated in anti-nuclear demonstrations.

Which is more likely?

1. Linda is a bank teller.
2. Linda is a bank teller and is active in the feminist movement.

Most people incorrectly answer this question. Can you think of the reason? When did you last fall prey to the conjunction fallacy?

More than 80 per cent of participants chose option 2, regardless of whether they were novice, intermediate or expert statisticians. However, the probability of two events occurring in conjunction is always less than or equal to the probability of either one occurring alone. Compare the Linda case to the following case: What is more likely, (1) you will have a flat tire tomorrow morning or (2) you will have a flat tire tomorrow and that a man in a black car will stop to help you out. In this case, it should be evident that (2) is not the most likely outcome.

Beware of the conjunction fallacy. It has deadly repercussions.

OVERFITTING

All of us have a natural tendency to think that more specific the information, the less likely it is to be wrong. Therefore, we implicitly assume that specific is more likely than general.

Overfitting is a statistical concept best understood by a quote attributed to Nobel Laureate Ronald Coase—'If you torture the data long enough, it will confess to anything.'

Our headaches do have some commonalities with the symptoms of brain tumour but believing that every headache is a tumour can lead to bouts of anxiety. This tendency to think that a headache is a tumour is how Overfitting creeps into our daily lives. We all do it in some shape or form.

While we should steer clear of Overfitting, we should be aware of the opposite scenario. Imagine you get strong bouts of headache every few days. Thinking it is not something serious can also have detrimental effects. In such a situation, it is best to consult a doctor.

For day-to-day stuff, especially things that matter, don't under or overfit. Learn to be driven by data and guided by intuition. With some training, you will learn the optimum balance.

FRAME OF REFERENCE

Framing refers to the way we present a situation so that our perspective is clearly understood.

We all tend to frame our point of view in a way that moves us closer to our intended outcome. There are three things we must keep in mind while framing.

First, our perspective is almost always biased. Neutrality is a particularly hard thing to achieve. Even when we are not saying something, we are communicating. When we choose to react to something and let another thing go by, our silence unwittingly communicates our stance.

Second, our perspective can wildly differ from the person we are framing the problem statement to.

Third, most of us are unclear about our intended outcome. When we argue on social media, what do we really want to accomplish?

What's our intended outcome? Do we want to change the other person's mind or prove that we are particularly knowledgeable about the issue at hand or both? Or is it that we are arguing because we are bored and have nothing better to do?

That is why it is so important to start with the intended outcome and work backwards. You might think that doing this will make the conversation dry, scripted and devoid of spontaneity. But I am not saying that you do this for all conversations. Just consider it for the ones where you are investing serious intellectual or emotional capital.

Once you have identified your goal, lay out the facts at hand emphasizing the 'why'. Author Simon Sinek shares that people don't care as much about what we are saying as they do about why we are saying it. Our framing of the problem should leverage first-principles and be fact-based as much as possible. However, we humans don't think in terms of facts. Our facts need to come together in a way that the listener or reader at least understands why they matter to us.

Many products and services we consume use framing all the time to influence us. Consider tweets, newspaper headlines and Instagram quotes. Poker player and author Maria Konnikova wrote an article titled *A Gene That Makes You Need Less Sleep?* Even by her own admission, it is not inaccurate in any way. But it does likely prompt focus on one specific part of the piece which nudges the reader to explore more.

We all use framing to our advantage by simply knowing this shared human trait can help us explore the essence of the matter at hand with open eyes.

ANCHORING

It describes our tendency to focus on the first piece of information while making decisions.

Marketers exploit Anchoring all the time to sell us less for more by making us believe we got a bargain. The idea is simple. Get our minds to subconsciously accept the fair value of a transaction and then play around within a range. Think back to your last conversation with your real estate broker or the used car salesman. The initial price he or she quotes sets the standard for the rest of the negotiations. If it is preposterous, most of us walk away but most sales people are smarter than that. They tend to have an intuitive idea of our willingness to play and they conduct micro A-B tests in real time. More often than not, they win, even if we think otherwise.

Since I am most interested in helping build meaningful careers, let's explore salary negotiations. In almost all cases, your offer letter has a salary mentioned. If you think it is less than you deserve, you go back to them. In turn they say that their hands are tied as they have a range to operate in and they gave you the highest possible one. You push more and they increase it by two per cent. You are happy as you think you got more. They are happy because they know they got you for less than their maximum allowable limit.

More than losing money, anchoring effect leads to consistently suboptimal decision-making. That's what you need to train yourself to avoid. Every time you are making a consequential decision or are part of an important negotiation, spot where the other party tried to anchor you and be ready for a counter. Make it punchy and let it be known, subtly, that you have power to walk away..

AVAILABILITY BIAS

Availability Bias is how our environment can shape our perceptions. Available information doesn't automatically imply legitimate information.

We are all deeply influenced by our network and our communities that tend to be composed of people like us. Diversity, even in our cherished communities, is often minimal. In a country like

India where one in eight people speak English, readers of this book are part of this articulate, loud, powerful yet in many ways, insignificant minority. We exaggerate what we know, we know far less than we think and what we know is at best a sliver of the truth.

All digital channels are screaming for our attention and are consciously or unconsciously trying to manipulate us. That's why it is important to get to diversify our sources of information. The easiest and most productive way to do it is to deliberately connect with those who do not think and dream like us. It will be hard to begin with but it will train our mind to overcome the tyranny of flickering instincts triggered by the first notification that pops on to our phone.

CHAPTER 64

THE ART OF FOOLING ONESELF

Knowing that we constantly fool ourselves is an important lesson in self-discovery.

DISTRUST EPIPHANIES: BE SCEPTICAL ABOUT EVOCATIVE STORIES USED TO SELL IDEAS

Isaac Newton sitting under the apple tree and Archimedes lounging in his bathing tub are memorable stories because they align with our romantic idea about inspiration and genius. The truth is far more complicated and often more boring than that.

Origin stories of companies often hinge on such evocative images only because they are memorable.

Netflix co-founder Marc Randolph explains that the idea of starting Netflix did not occur in a divine moment of inspiration. It had nothing to do with the much talked about late fee that Reed Hastings (the other co-founder) did not want to pay. In fact, at the beginning, much like their key competitor Blockbuster, Netflix charged a similar late fee.

So how was Netflix born? It was a result of working through and thinking about hundreds of ideas over long car rides that Randolph and Hastings took together. The timing, choice of industry, team, etc., were important but the key element was the perfect product-market-founder fit.

So, what is the key insight for you? Forget epiphanies. If you want to come up with better ideas, come up with more ideas. Sometimes it will be hard to differentiate between good and bad ideas but the exercise is worth it, especially at the initial stages of a project.

Randolph adds that the best ideas make themselves apparent with time. Once you stumble upon an interesting idea, keep in mind that it will evolve and so will you, your team the environment you live in.

Even the greatest of ideas need tweaking, tinkering and adapting.

FEYNMAN PRINCIPLE

'The first principle is that you must not fool yourself and you are the easiest person to fool.'

Richard Feynman's quote is as applicable to careers as to life. That is why we must continually ask ourselves tough questions every three months. Are we solving a problem or inventing a problem to solve? Are we creating an impact or pretending to do so? Impact can be social, financial, business, technical or creative but it must be measurable. If we can't quantify our impact, we must be able to visualize a stakeholder or a shareholder whose life we made marginally better through our work. Not being able to quantify impact or visualize a shareholder/stakeholder is a red flag. If you are in your current pursuit to build your resume, good luck! You will need a lot of it as 'luck' is your strategy.

Whenever someone calls me/meets me for career/grad school advice, I ask them the following questions:

1. What do you do?
2. Why do you do what you do? (Subtext: What motivates you?)
3. Walk me through a day at work.
4. What is the impact you have had?

5. What problem(s) are you most inspired to solve?
6. Will your next professional step take you closer to the problem you wish to solve?

Problem can be social, technical, business, creative or financial. There is no hierarchy of problems.

Resume-driven people often give answers that sound like concatenation of buzzwords. Impact-driven people give clear answers because their motivation is intrinsic. They are driven by solving problems creatively as opposed to preparing to solve problems one fine day when all chips fall in place. Truth be told, all chips never fall in place.

We need to start small, dream big and live in the present.

Three points to keep in mind are:

1. Reflect on your internal motivation. There is NO substitute for that and you can't FAKE it.
2. Solid impact creates a pretty CV. It does NOT work the other way around.
3. You must not fool yourself and you are the easiest person to fool.

ESCALATION OF COMMITMENT

Escalation of Commitment is a human behavioural pattern in which an individual or group facing increasingly negative outcomes from a decision, action or investment nevertheless continues the behaviour instead of altering course. We maintain behaviour that is irrational, but aligns with our previous decisions and actions both in professional and personal lives.

Status quo is comfortable even if we know that it is hurting us. Even if a project/investment/idea/relationship backfired, we continue engaging till the very end and sometimes even after. We expect miracles to happen and drastic changes to occur but they rarely do

(Miracles do occur but since many of us expect miracles, statistics make things complicated). All we are left with is the regret of a poor decision and its long hangover, over and above the obvious loss of money, time and mental peace.

All of this said, we all escalate commitments on a regular basis. We tell ourselves a known devil is better than an unknown angel and go on with the usual song and dance.

If you want to disrupt the alchemy of forces shaping your thought process, you must be willing to walk away. That is the only way to negotiate an alternate outcome. The negotiation is not only with the other party but also with yourself and that is the hardest part. How do you walk away from a decision that you made (at least in principle) as a fully functional, sentient being?

I feel the answer is three-fold. First, have low expectations. Second, track those expectations backwards (relying on past information) and forward (projecting two cycles ahead). Third, know yourself. If you are ok with taking gambles and nurturing ambiguity, go right ahead. If the very thought of this leaves you sweating, walk away now.

It all comes down to negotiations—if you are not willing to walk away, you will not have a fair outcome.

BOILING FROG SYNDROME

The boiling frog is a fable describing a frog being slowly boiled alive. The premise is that if a frog is put suddenly into boiling water, it will jump out, but if the frog is put in tepid water which is then brought to a boil slowly, it will not perceive the danger and will be cooked to death.

I think all of us are the boiling frog in different situations. We are engineered to at least try and avoid emergencies and unexpected situations. However, we tend to ignore our habits, micro-behaviours, biases that over time become an integral part of our personality. These ignored behavioural patterns lead to self-inflicted misery.

The biggest challenge of grappling with boiling frog syndrome is diagnosing the root cause. Let's analyse how most professionals begin their work day. They sleep next to a phone that keeps buzzing through the night. They wake up to hundreds of mails and notifications, and get into the respond-and-react mode. By the time they are done responding to the seemingly urgent requests for attention, their mind is sapped of energy and vitality. The quality of the whole day is compromised. This impacts creativity and even interferes with how meaningful people find their work. This digital addiction didn't happen overnight. We kept increasing our digital consumption daily. Everything in life is about compound interest. Micro-improvements every day make us richer, fitter and happier. Micro-deteriorations every day make us addicts.

Think of anything that you have become better or worse at. It will be a result of micro-changes. Eighty per cent of our misery comes from 20 per cent of micro-deteriorations. Just reflect on the past few years and figure out the top three things that have brought you down. Visualize the correlations with the boiling frog who didn't see it coming or rather who knowingly ignored the facts and kept adjusting till he could adjust no more.

BUTTERFLY EFFECT

Sensitive dependence on initial conditions in which a small change in one state results in large differences in a later state.

Technology, economy, weather, voting patterns, etc., are chaotic systems. While we can predict trends, it is almost impossible to know the long-term state. Mathematician Edward Lorenz spent his life trying to analyse such chaotic systems and is rightly considered the pioneer of chaos theory.

Lorenz popularized the phrase Butterfly Effect and defined it as the sensitive dependence on initial conditions in which a small change in one state can result in large differences in a later state. He explained by stating that the path of a tornado can be affected by a butterfly flapping its wings weeks before. Let's explore his explanation: The butterfly flaps its wings, thereby sending the air particles on a slightly divergent path. It gets amplified over time and ultimately results in a different path for the tornado.

Our life, even in the most peaceful phase, is a chaotic system. That is why adaptability is so important. In her TED Talk, Goldman Sachs's, Natalie Fratto explains how AQ (adaptability quotient) is a defining measure of intelligence, and accurately predicts chances of success in this unpredictable era.

AQ is how well a person reacts to change and is something that can be measured, tested and improved. Whether you are a writer, a scientist, a musician, a business school aspirant or a postman, you will witness unprecedented change multiple times in your life. By working on your AQ, you will not only learn to negotiate with change but also to make it your biggest ally.

To my mind, unlearning is the most defining aspect of high AQ. This is especially hard when you are good at something but that something undergoes a massive change. Let us take trading as an example. The profession attracts people with high IQ, great quantitative skills and strong work ethic. They train themselves to manage stress and respond to the twists and turns of the market through math and tricks of the trade learned over time. Over the years, there has been a huge shift in the way this industry works. Tasks previously assigned to smart traders are moving on to smart algorithms. It is possible that almost all of trading is outsourced to machines. What should a trader, a high-income high skill professional do to adapt to the new structure?

It is hard to predict the exact changes in any industry but the fact that change is coming is not up for debate. The pace of change will be surprising and even the best of us will be left high and dry if we don't spend time unlearning the very aspects of ourselves that made us successful.

What worked in the past will no longer hold true. This does not mean that all your past efforts are wasted. All that it implies is that it needs to be channelled and reinforced in a different direction.

SHIRKY PRINCIPLE

The mental model 'Shirky Principle' states that institutions will try to preserve the problem to which they are the solution. If you grew up in a developing country, you have seen the Shirky Principle in full swing at your school or university or local government office.

Clay Shirky is an adjunct professor in New York University's graduate *Interactive Telecommunications Program*, where he teaches a course named 'Social Weather'. His work focuses on the rising usefulness of networks—using decentralized technologies such as peer-to-peer sharing that enable new kinds of cooperative structures. As things progress, people find ways of getting things done in business, science, the arts and elsewhere, as an alternative to centralized and institutional structures, which he sees as self-limiting.

Does the phrase 'this is how it is done' ring a bell? It is the classic refrain of those who have actively contributed to first creating the problem, then exacerbating it and are now exclusive gatekeepers of propriety and order.

Sometimes they invoke nostalgia and sometimes they paint colourful images of an impending doom. They selectively draw upon lessons of the past and paint a dystopian picture. They want your fear to cloud your judgement. They are not the least bit interested in solving your problem. Why? Because that will make them irrelevant. Such people invoke status quo as a strategy.

In some cases, maintaining order or keeping things the way they are is essential to analyse all aspects of the issue. Bad strategy can be worse than no strategy at all.

That said, if your strategy is to preserve a problem so that you can exclusively solve it, you are embodying Shirky Principle.

LUCK SURFACE AREA

$L = D \times T$, where 'L' is luck, 'D' is doing and 'T' is telling.

Serial entrepreneur Jason Roberts inadvertently coined the phrase 'Luck Surface Area'. It turns out that it popped out of his mouth during a discussion episode of his podcast *TechZing*. Roberts explains that we can hack serendipity and make ourselves lucky. Instead of being subject to the whims and fancies of luck, we can create our destiny. Here is how it works.

Luck Surface Area is directly proportional to the degree to which you do something you're passionate about combined with the total number of people to whom this is effectively communicated.

It is important to keep in mind that passion is not enough. However, we tend to work harder for things we truly care about. Because our work is channelled, the output per hour is greater and we become much better. As we get better, more people get to know about what we are doing and they tell their friends. Network effects set it. At this stage, we can let things be and take their natural course or we can proactively reach out to those who can be catalysts for our mission. Companies or missions that truly make a difference are driven by men and women who get really good at their craft and effectively tell their story to a broad set of stakeholders.

Our friends knowing about our work isn't enough. We need to reach out to different networks, communities and organizations. New opportunities often come from surprising places. We call such happenstances serendipity but actually it is merely the expansion of our Luck Surface Area.

FLYWHEEL

Flywheel is a rotating disk that stores energy. Remember the merry-go-round in school or your neighbourhood park? That is basically a flywheel. It takes quite an effort to start spinning but once it gains momentum, it takes minimal effort to sustain.

It is a concept popularized by author Jim Collins who is known for inviting Steve Jobs to teach his business school class.

He explains:

> No matter how dramatic the end result, good-to-great transformations never happen in one fell swoop. In building a great company or social sector enterprise, there is no single defining action, no grand program, no one killer innovation, no solitary lucky break, no miracle moment. Rather, the process resembles relentlessly pushing a giant, heavy flywheel, turn upon turn, building momentum until a point of breakthrough, and beyond.

In day-to-day life, you will observe that it takes ages to become an expert at something or build something but once we push ourselves to a certain level, it takes minimal effort to stay on top.

Let's try and visualize it with the help of networks. Say you move to a new city or a new country or a different industry, it is likely that you have to put an inordinate effort and time in getting to know people and be part of interesting networks.

However, once you have put in the initial effort and built a reputation, you will find it much easier to blend in. Each new person you get to know and add value to strengthens the momentum of your flywheel. All you need to do is focus on sincere, micro efforts that over time compound to something meaningful.

The beauty of the Flywheel mental model is that it makes tough problems seem solvable and provides perspective into our daily struggles. Perhaps our efforts are taking us closer to a state where things get easier, more fun and more rewarding.

ENTROPY

Entropy is the measure of disorder in any system. In any closed system, it does not decrease on its own.

I am not about to trouble you with physics right now but use the principle of Entropy to explain how you should channel your time and think about your relationships.

Orderliness/terms/systems need to be maintained, else they wither away inch by inch, without you even realizing. Do you remember days that end up becoming randomized with micro-distractions? That is basically Entropy at display.

Similarly relationships don't fall apart one fine day. The randomness keeps increasing—slowly but surely—till they become unrecognizable.

One of the interesting things Network Capital community members have all done is that we have scaled trust across cities, countries and religions. Now that the trust is built and the brand established, can we sit back and chill?

If we do, Entropy will destroy us. We need to reinvest in the relationships that helped us get to this point. To maintain the same level of trust with our community members, we need to keep building on it. The most practical way to build trust is to help others by adding value to what they most care about.

This is the trust equation popularized by the book *The Trusted Adviser.*

Trust = (Credibility + Reliability + Intimacy)/Self-orientation

In a way, this trust equation is what makes peer mentoring work for Network Capital. We count on each other's credibility, reliability and willingness to make us feel safe in order to arrive at a win-win scenario for all of us.

Now let us explore Entropy and productivity by looking at how we pay attention. Entropy tells us that if we are not mindful of our day, it will keep getting more random every hour. We need to train our mind to focus on things that really move the needle.

While we keep the mental model of Entropy in mind, we should also remember to research on the value of messiness on our lives. Basically, controlled chaos can foster creativity.

The key word here is controlled. That is how you need to manage entropy else entropy will manage you.

GAMBLER'S FALLACY

The Gambler's Fallacy, also known as the Monte Carlo fallacy, is the mistaken belief that if something happens more frequently than normal during a given period, it will happen less frequently in the future (or vice versa).

Let me take you back to the Monte Carlo Casino in the year 1913.

On 18 August 1913, a casino in Monte Carlo (Monaco) had an extremely improbable run of 26 blacks. You know the probability of that happening? It is one in 137 million. Legend has it that the best of gamblers lost millions of francs betting against black. They thought that since there have been so many sequences of black that the next one has to be red. There is absolutely no reason for them to think so but such is the power of misguided intuition.

Monte Carlo fallacy is at work any and everywhere sequential decisions are involved, including but not limited to getting a loan approved or disapproved, a guilty or not guilty verdict in court or even decisions in cricket. Have you ever observed the three or four consecutive leg-before-wicket decisions? I haven't. In my GRE exam, I distinctly remember feeling quite nervous when the first five maths questions had option 'D' as the correct response. I thought maybe I was making a mistake. It seemed quite unlikely that the test makers had designed the first five questions that way. There was no rational reason for me to think so but it crossed my mind. Thankfully, I didn't succumb to the whims of Monte Carlo fallacy but I came close enough.

University of Chicago decided to review asylum cases between the years 1985 and 2013. It turns out that highly accomplished judges were less likely to grant asylum if they had approved the last two.

The way to apply Gambler's Fallacy to real life is simple—don't expect short-term results to match long-term expectations and don't base long-term expectations on a small number of short-term results. Both entrepreneurs and VCs should think long and hard about the implications of Gambler's Fallacy.

Warren Buffet's mentor Benjamin Graham explained poetically: In the short run, the market is like a voting machine—tallying up which firms are popular and unpopular. But in the long run, the market is like a weighing machine—assessing the substance of a company.

CHAPTER 65

SHARPENING HOW WE THINK

In a world filled with distractions and stimulations, we can seek comfort in timeless truths that bring focus to our work and life at large.

METCALFE'S LAW

Strength of a network is the square of its trusted connections (nodes).

Network Capital started off as a cross-border mentoring project. I thought if young people from countries that have vastly different political and economic ideologies mentor each other, the world will be more connected and more united than ever before. Our mentor–mentee pairs included India–Pakistan, Russia–Ukraine, Israel–Palestine, United States–Russia to name a few. While the thesis proved to be true and we had powerful cross-border stories to share, the impact and growth was incremental. We were trying to change the world one mentoring pair at a time.

What saved us was the peer mentoring and skill-sharing culture, powered by Metcalfe's Law, which basically states that the power of a network goes up with the square of the people on that network. We ensured that every single person joining our network was whetted and reviewed so we were able to scale the trust and overall network efficacy exponentially. This was critically important as the underlying premise of Metcalfe's Law is that every node of the network has the same value for the network. While we cannot ensure that each of our members is equally matched in skills and accomplishments, we can definitely optimize for either of the two factors—hunger to learn or willingness to share.

While both these metrics are fairly intangible, we can get a sense of it through our application form or peer referral system. By ensuring zero spam and zero toxicity, we were able to give wings to the Metcalfe Law.

CRITICAL MASS

Critical Mass is defined as the size, number or an amount large enough to produce a particular result. The fax machine was invented in the 1840s but it only became mainstreamed in the 1970s when enough number of people started using them.

In business, Kevin Kelley's concept of 1,000 true fans offers a useful formula for achieving critical mass and building things that scale. In today's world, every business is basically some version of a subscription business. People are owning less and subscribing more—be it homes, cars, IT services, streaming options, etc.

Kelley explains that to be a successful creator, you don't need millions. You don't need millions of dollars or millions of customers, millions of clients or millions of fans. To make a living as a craftsperson, photographer, musician, designer, author, animator, app maker, entrepreneur, or inventor, you need only 1,000 true fans. He defines a true fan as a fan that will buy anything you produce.

For the true power of 1,000 true fans to set in, we need two conditions to be satisfied. First, you have to create enough each year so that you can earn, on average, USD 100 profit from each true fan. Second, you must have a direct relationship with your fans.

1,000 true fans × USD 100 = USD 100,000 which is more than the living cost of most people. But the fun part is that the story doesn't stop at 1,000 fans. Our true fans create a strong pull for other users to join the inner circle thereby expanding the fan base.

Also, thinking about a thousand is far more practical than thinking about millions and billions. Once we get to the critical mass of 1,000, millions might be a by-product but if we don't hit a thousand, thinking about millions can only be intimidating.

While in this section we focused more on the positive scenarios, sinister ideas and ideologies also reach critical mass and inflict societies at scale. In fact, technology only accelerates them. The answer to such negative proliferation also lies in communities united in creating resistance. These resistance communities also need to reach a critical mass to offer a viable alternative and an answer to the negative forces.

CORRELATION CAUSATION DANCE

Don't confuse correlation with causation.

Life is whimsically beautiful and confusing. Consider the following analysis done by Tyler Vigen:

1. US spending on science, space and technology has a 99.79 per cent correlation with suicides by hanging, strangulation and suffocation.
2. Per capita cheese consumption has a 94.71 per cent correlation with number of people who died by becoming tangled in their bedsheets.
3. Divorce rate in Maine has a 99.26 per cent correlation with per capita consumption of margarine.
4. Total revenue generated by arcades has a 98.5 per cent correlation with computer science doctorates in the United States.
5. Per capita consumption of mozzarella cheese has a 95.86 per cent correlation with civil engineering doctorates.

6. Per capita consumption of chicken has a 90 per cent correlation with total US crude oil imports.
7. Number of people who drowned in a swimming pool has a 90 per cent correlation with power generated by US nuclear power plants.
8. Letters in winning words of spelling bee have an 80 per cent correlation with the number of people killed by venomous spiders.

Tyler is a military intelligence analyst and a Harvard Law student who demonstrates the golden rule that 'correlation does not equal causation' with the help of beautiful graphs.

While in many of the above-mentioned cases, it is easy to understand the difference between correlation and causation, in some cases things can get really tricky. The consumption of margarine is most likely not leading to divorces in Maine even though the correlation is more than 99 per cent. Intuitively it makes sense but what explains the spike in divorces in March and August? Is it random or is there a cause?

In everyday life, we make tons of mistakes interchanging correlation with causation. The key lesson is that we must learn to temper our intuition. Sometimes the unlikeliest scenarios result from each other and sometimes seemingly connected events are nothing more than random interplays.

UNKNOWN–UNKNOWNS

Absence of evidence is not evidence of absence.

This became popular with United States Secretary of Defence Donald Rumsfield in the year 2002.

> Reports that say that something hasn't happened are always interesting to me, because as we know, there are known knowns; there are things we know we know. We also know

there are known unknowns; that is to say we know there are some things we do not know. But there are also unknown unknowns—the ones we don't know we don't know. And if one looks throughout the history of our country and other free countries, it is the latter category that tend to be the difficult ones.

The absence of evidence is not evidence of absence, or vice versa.

A related concept is Johari Window which is a technique that helps people better understand their relationship with themselves and others. It was created by psychologists Joseph Luft (1916–2014) and Harrington Ingham (1916–1995) in the year 1955, and is used primarily in self-help groups and corporate settings as a heuristic exercise.

The Johari window has four quadrants, that represent four combinations:

- Open Space: Known to you–Known to others.
- Blind Spot: Unknown to yourself–Known to others.
- Hidden Area: Known to yourself–Unknown to others.
- Unknown Area: Unknown to yourself–Unknown to others.

We should always watch out for our blind spots.

Imagine someone who speaks really well. He always has interesting things to add and powerful stories to recount. It is possible that this unchecked reliance on public speaking could lead to incomplete development of other skills, say writing or critical thinking. It is also possible that he speaks so much and so well that his presence in the room leads other people to become too self-conscious. In the end, they end up resenting him.

Blind spots are hard to identify. We need a core group of trusted confidants who make us aware of our behavioural patterns and caution us. This won't happen automatically. We need to consciously put effort into it.

RADICAL CANDOUR

Radical Candour is when a person cares for your growth and simultaneously presents a direct challenge.

Investor Nassim Nicholas Taleb predicted the 2008 financial crisis and alluded to the Coronavirus outbreak way back in 2007, in his bestseller *The Black Swan*. Taleb owes his professional success to spotting unlikely trends and sharing uncomfortable truths. I often wonder if he is an effective communicator because he is abrasive or despite it?

Simply telling uncomfortable the truths isn't enough. We need to ensure that the underlying message reaches the intended audience effectively. CEO coach Kim Scott has developed a four-pronged behavioural awareness framework to effectively guide important conversations. It is worth keeping in mind that these are behaviours (not personality types) that all of us fall into from time to time.

First, Radical Candour. It is a management philosophy when a person cares for your growth and simultaneously presents a direct challenge. Scott learned it first-hand from Facebook COO Sheryl Sandberg who used to be her manager at Google. After a largely successful presentation, Sandberg asked Scott to walk with her. She shared that Scott needed a speaking coach to avoid awkward pauses.

To Scott it seemed like a trivial point. She listened but it was clear she wasn't going to act on the feedback. Finally, Sheryl said, 'You know, Kim, I can tell I'm not really getting through to you. I'm going to have to be clearer here. When you say "um" every third word, it makes you sound stupid.'

According to Scott, Sandberg's Radical Candour was the kindest thing she could have done for her professional growth. There are four defining aspects of Radical Candour—it is humble, helpful, immediate and in-person if it's criticism and in public if it's praise.

In a high trust environment, Radical Candour works like a charm. However, Radical Candour requires training. You first have to establish that you care for the person you are offering feedback to. Only after that can you expect to offer sharp critique and still manage to have a healthy relationship.

Further, obnoxious aggression occurs when we challenge someone directly, but don't establish that we care about them. This is most commonly observed when someone with leverage and credibility publicly shames or mocks others to get the outcome he wants. While the aggressor might feel powerful in the short term, it is a guaranteed way to not get the outcome he wants in a longer timeframe.

In today's connected world, the way we treat people is public knowledge. We might have some leverage today, but nothing is permanent. People never forget the way we make them feel. As an obnoxious aggressor, one should keep in mind that we are making ourselves unemployable in the long term.

Third, manipulative sincerity is the hallmark of toxic cultures. This is often an after effect of obnoxious aggression and leads to a situation when we neither care nor challenge. Insincere praise, flattery and back stabbing are commonly observed traits of manipulative sincerity.

Last is ruinous empathy. It is what happens when we want to spare someone's feelings in the short term and end up not telling them something they absolutely need to know. We care but fail to challenge. Ruinous empathy may feel safe, but is ultimately damaging. Empathy is a great asset but it can paralyze us if we prioritize relational comfort over what is good for the other person. Scott shares that 85 per cent of management mistakes are a direct result of ruinous empathy.

After years of studying and analysing Taleb's writings, I have come to the conclusion that he straddles the fine line between Radical Candour and obnoxious aggression. Perhaps he can get away with it given his age and experience. But for us millennials, adopting radical candour as default communication style is the most rational option and we should consider it.

POTEMKIN VILLAGE

It is a literal or figurative construction built solely to deceive others into thinking that a situation is better than it really is.

The term comes from stories of a fake portable village built to impress Empress Catherine II by her former lover Grigory Potemkin, during her journey to Crimea in the year 1787. Legend has it that Potemkin erected temporary portable settlements along the banks of the Dnieper River in order to impress the Russian Empress. The structures were part of an elaborate charade to signal strength and accomplishment.

This model is useful to identify when a politician, a business leader or an activist is trying to make you believe in something that doesn't exist or is unlikely to come true. While you can occasionally tell when someone is taking you for a ride, we aren't great at figuring out Potemkin Village like situations.

Instead of focusing on the promise versus delivery ratio of our leaders, we tend to get swayed by impassioned speeches, colourful advertisements and exaggerated assertions.

Things get more complicated when a person/entity with a reasonably strong promise versus delivery ratio decides to build a Potemkin Village. Think of Wall Street in the year 2008 when an entire industry decided to build a Potemkin Village, knowing that you are likely to trust them. They had been successful on several occasions. How might we think of spotting scenarios like that?

I like to call it the 'Get Rich Quick' framework. Anytime you hear of something that seems too good to be true, you should be ultra-cautious. It is probably not your—about to get rich quickly—moment, rather, it is most likely someone trying to get rich by exploiting you, investor Naval Ravikant explained in his podcast.

All of this said, one must learn to distinguish a positive, can-do attitude from a Potemkin Village. Many times, individuals and organizations project an image of strength as a signalling value—either to the market or to their internal stakeholders. As long as it is designed to propel actual performance, it isn't a Potemkin Village. If it is put together as a cover up, it is just a matter of time before it blows up.

'YET EACH MAN KILLS THE THING HE LOVES': IT IS YOU...

This quote comes from Oscar Wilde who was an Anglo-Irish playwright, novelist, poet and critic. Mental models emerge from myriad themes and trace their origin to wildly interesting combination of knowledge systems. Let's see what Wilde had to say about self-sabotage.

To understand this mental model, try and think of something that was most treasured, someone who mattered more than others, something you built your life with all your heart and soul—but who doesn't exist today. It is part of your history, one that you may or may not remember fondly.

Now comes the hard part. I am sure you don't think you had a role in ruining your relationship with that person and you won't be entirely wrong. However, just as a thought experiment, think of the instances where a different reaction/approach/coping method could have yielded a different outcome. An honest afternoon with yourself will reveal that in almost every case, you ended what you cherished most. If that seems harsh, think of it as you being a co-conspirator in the outcome.

This mental model isn't meant to take you on a guilt trip, quite the opposite. It is meant to reveal that each of us has a tendency for self-sabotage and most importantly, that we can mitigate it.

When we get too attached to an outcome, we get blinded. It is a lot like a drunk racer trying to get to the finish line as soon as possible.

That is why the next time you viscerally get attached to an outcome, know that you might just kill it. Take a pause, go for a walk and remember all you need to do is to get out of your way.

WISDOM OF CROWDS

Crowds are reservoirs of insights and ideas. We just need to create the right culture, context and incentives to draw the best out of them and add unique value to them.

In the year 2009, Netflix held a contest to get ideas from literally anyone interested to beat its own recommendation algorithm. The 'Netflix Prize' was an open competition for the best collaborative filtering algorithm to predict user ratings for films, based on previous ratings without any other information.

As you can imagine Netflix had the best of researchers, academicians and computer scientists working for it. However, a team of external research scientists working part time to accomplish the goal beat Netflix's algorithm by a big margin of 10.06 per cent. On September 21 2009, the grand prize of USD 1,000,000 was given to the eBellKor's Pragmatic Chaos team.

Although, at the time, Netflix did not end up using the algorithm due to engineering and cost considerations, the contest demonstrated the power of crowdsourcing. Since then large and small organizations have consistently leveraged the power of crowdsourcing to solve problems.

At the core of it, Network Capital leverages wisdom of crowds (trusted and verified) for career advice and professional upskilling.

With every post, you get a wide range of answers and suggestions on the topics that interest you. It helps you get feedback from trusted advisors with experience you may not have. As we have discussed in previous mental models, it empowers you to uncover unknown unknowns and known unknowns.

That said, according to extensive research on wisdom of crowds, slightly different conditions are optimum to get the most out of such contexts. Author James Surowiecki's seminal book begins with the story of a 1906 county fair where almost 800 people participated to guess the weight of an Ox. Each of them made their individual guesses and the average weight was spot on—1197 pounds.

Isn't it miraculous?

According to Surowiecki, there are three conditions that must be met for wisdom of crowds to work.

First, diversity of opinion. We need to draw upon the individual knowledge of a large number of people.

Second, independence. These people must not let their opinions influence one another. You will notice that this does not happen during exit polls or actual voting during elections. There is a reason why exit polls are consistently wrong.

On Network Capital, we replace independence with inter-dependence. We want each of our hundreds of thousands of members to have independent insights on career but we also want to encourage meaningful dialogue and discussion. That is why we pay such close emphasis on content curation and profile verification. Each Network Capital member is vetted and verified. We don't want us to become a large club or a clique but to become the world's largest community of trusted, verified advisers. When we comment on each other's questions or suggest ideas, we are in a way influencing decisions of not only the person asking for advice but also all the people who have provided advice. This also includes people who go through all posts without commenting. They are influenced as well. That's the point of departure from what Surowiecki suggests.

Lastly, assimilation. The organization, entity or community doing the crowdsourcing needs to assimilate diverse opinions and ideas thoughtfully in order to arrive at a collective decision. That is why on Network Capital, we conduct office hours, mentoring sessions, masterclasses and offline meets. We want to empower our members to develop frameworks and mental models that are able to distinguish between music and noise.

To sum up, crowds are reservoirs of insights and ideas. We just need to create the right culture, context and incentives to draw the best out of them and add unique value to them.

RASHOMON EFFECT

The Rashomon Effect refers to an instance when the same event is described in significantly different (often contradictory) ways by different people who are involved.

Anne Duke, the author of *Thinking in Bets* writes,

> We've all experienced situations where we get two accounts of the same event, but the versions are dramatically different because they're informed by different facts and perspectives. This is known as Rashomon Effect, named for the 1950 cinematic classic Rashomon, directed by Akira Kurosawa. The central element of the otherwise simple plot was how incompleteness is a tool for bias. In the film, four people give separate, drastically different accounts of a scene they all observed, the seduction (or rape) of a woman by a bandit, the bandit's duel with her husband (if there was a duel), and the husband's death (from losing the duel, murder, or suicide).

These days, in all aspects of our lives, Rashomon Effect is in full swing. Just try and scroll through your social media or switch TV channels after a newsworthy event. It can be deeply unsettling when there are multiple versions of facts floating around. On top of that, we have loud commentators and clickbait advertising designed to obfuscate the truth. How are we supposed to make sense of the world when contradictory data and insights are thrown around with the sole vision to confuse us?

I subscribe to technology forecaster Paul Saffo's decision-making framework called *Strong Opinions, Weakly Held*. Paul suggests that despite lack of available information, we should develop a strong, fact-based hypothesis. Conviction is an important decision-making tool, but it shouldn't blind us. We should continually gather information that either supports or refutes our hypothesis. If we uncover information unfriendly to our beliefs, we should abandon our beliefs. That doesn't make us flaky. If anything, it shows maturity. Clinging to our idea in the face of contradictory information is the origin of most bad decisions.

DIFFUSION OF RESPONSIBILITY: NO DIRECTLY RESPONSIBLE INDIVIDUAL (DRI), NO OUTCOME

Almost every Diwali, there is a huge outcry against air pollution in Delhi. The government, political opposition, corporates, students, activists, start-ups and journalists are all outraged against the woeful state of affairs in one of the largest cities in the world. Although, this outrage and outcry helps in raising awareness about the challenge, not much comes out of it. Have you ever wondered why?

To answer this question, one has to explore what goes on at Apple Inc., specifically the concept of DRI which stands for Directly Responsible Individual.

As Gloria Lin who worked at Apple explains, it is a simple tool to make ownership clear and point people with questions to the right place. It's not a process or framework for project management.

They have DRIs on everything including from major initiatives to bug reports which end up clarifying a lot of questions of ownership, liability and accountability.

Gloria Lin explains when DRI matters the most. Once you read her thesis, you will appreciate and draw parallels to the air pollution problem.

1. When solving a complex, cross-functional issue;
2. When it's unclear who's got the ball and what should be happening; and
3. When everyone knows that something is important, but no one feels like it's their responsibility to see it through all the way.

Having a DRI also saves collective team energy and efficiency by ensuring that everyone is not worrying about the same problem. Different individuals and teams are doing their bit and things will come together.

Even if you work in an organization where there aren't many systems and processes, you must consider DRI, else some people will end up (unsuccessfully) trying to solve many parts of the problem and some who do nothing more than pretending to work (you will be surprised by how many such people exist).

Armed with the DRI framework, you can easily understand which problems will be solved and which ones would remain unsolved where people collectively get outraged till they find something else to direct their outrage towards.

Saying that DRI doesn't work because the problem is too complex is not acceptable. In fact, if the problem is complex, like air pollution, you need DRI even more—a person who is accountable for outcomes, not sound-bites. I wonder if we will ever see this in politics but that is one field where we desperately need a DRI.

Having attended and spoken at hundreds of government and multilateral meetings, I can give you a simple rule of thumb that is equally applicable to start-ups and corporates: No DRI, no outcome.

HOFSTADTER'S LAW

'It always takes longer than you expect, even when you take into account Hofstadter's Law.'

Douglas Richard Hofstadter is a distinguished Professor of Cognitive Science and Comparative Literature at Indiana University. His book *Gödel, Escher, Bach: An Eternal Golden Braid*, first published in the year 1979, won both the Pulitzer Prize for general non-fiction and the National Book Award for Science.

Although Douglas Hofstadter is nominally associated with a few departments at Indiana University, he is actually left pretty much alone to pursue his multifarious interests, which he does with alacrity, celerity, vim, vigour and vitality. Hofstadter's own way of characterizing his personal style and his personal goals runs as follows: 'perpetually in search of beauty'.

In addition to his considerable achievements in science, he can also be credited for being the originator of Hofstadter's Law that makes the observation, 'It always takes longer than you expect, even when you take into account Hofstadter's Law.'

The essence of this law is that we are terrible at managing our time and attention. As discussed earlier when describing the Eisenhower Matrix, every important task isn't urgent and every urgent task isn't important.

Hofstadter's Law explains why despite our terrible track record in keeping to deadlines, we tend to flood our calendars with commitments.

I always worry when people describe how busy they are. Being busy isn't a sign of productivity. If anything, it is a sign of multiple things on your plate that are likely to take much longer than you had scheduled. More time juggling multiple things means that you don't have enough time to recharge and be at your best to take the decisions that actually matter, ones that move the needle.

The practical tip to deal with Hofstadter's Law is to allocate 20 per cent more time for high-value, high-impact activities that you perform. You don't want to rush through something critical just to make time for something that is urgent but unimportant.

For example, if you are a sales person, you want to prioritize high value deals and assign extra time for them. Knowing Hofstadter's Law, you will probably need it. That said, all of us have a long list of things we need to do in order to function. These are the things that you want to complete quickly, ideally in batches (for example, social emails that you need to return).

In a way, Hofstadter's Law isn't about time management. It is about prioritization. Taken in conjunction with Eisenhower Matrix, it can really help you make the most of the day/week/month.

CHAPTER 66

THE LAST LAP

In addition to these mental models, you should keep the following concepts in mind. They are operating principles that I have learned from interesting people doing interesting things. Sometimes they fail and sometimes they fall but their life lessons are important teachers for us.

LET FIRES BURN

One of my mentors explained the rule of eight to me. When confronted with crisis situations, let them be. Ninety per cent of them will vanish in no time. Reid Hoffman and the PayPal mafia also had a similar philosophy in the early days of establishing the company. They prioritized strategic product and company goals over immediate customer complaints.

Is it even fathomable to you that an early stage company with huge incumbents will ignore irate customers to make measurable organizational progress? This approach is obviously not for everyone. It requires a deep level of focus and conviction: focus to keep an eye on the ball and conviction that the short-term pain is worth the long-term gain.

I think letting non-urgent fires burn is one of the most important criteria for success, especially if you are in a role where you are paid to take key strategic decisions. When you decide to do something, there is always an opportunity cost—something business school teaches you well. You could choose to do a million other things at the same time. But should you?

The answer is a big fat no unless these conditions are met: Your family/friends need you; you are uniquely positioned to quench the fire; or your micro-intervention can enable your team to keep focus.

Let most fires burn. More often than not, they are illusions or distractions. The real challenges often come unannounced with full fury. You want to be prepared when that happens.

MEASURE WHAT MATTERS

Framing the right set of goals and measuring them persistently is the difference between raw success and profound failure. I believe that the objectives and key results (OKR) approach is a huge creativity and efficacy multiplier even at a personal level.

I want to use the next few paragraphs explaining why this is hard and how you should approach it. Let's begin by asking how you evaluate a day well spent? For me, it is usually a mix of spending time with my loved ones, reading, coaching Network Capital community members, connecting with old friends, going for a run and most importantly finding something to look forward to the next day. Quite a list, isn't it?

Everything mentioned above matters to me and adds meaning to my life. But the question still remains—what should my OKRs be?

After a lot of trial and error, I realized that keeping lists made things unmanageable. Focusing on three key goals at a time brought about much needed order to my work life.

Towards this end, I have been inspired by Warren Buffet. He says that to figure out what you want to pursue, list out your top 25 goals and then strike out all but three. That's your set of the most critical objectives. Now is the time to match your objectives with the top 3 key results you want.

It is possible that they do not converge. If that's the case, you need to go back to the exercise and figure out the disconnect. After a few tries, most of you will have a beautiful, reasonably well correlated list of strategic objectives and key results. Treat it like your mental GPS. It will guide you well.

TRUST TRILOGY

A Harvard Business School professor, Frances Frei, explains that our authenticity, logic or empathy can get in the way of someone trusting us. Let's explore each of these variables.

1. *Authenticity:* It is the difference between who we are and who we project to be. Being ourselves is easy among people who like us or who we relate to. It is challenging in unfamiliar settings. No matter what the setting, if people feel that we are being less than authentic, they don't trust us. The reaction is almost instinctive. Yes, our instincts can be wrong but most people still trust or distrust someone based on how they feel at that moment.

2. *Logic:* If the people don't buy our logic, they will never trust us. To ensure that our logic is watertight, one should stress test our hypothesis and communicate it clearly. As Dr Frei points out, most people fall short in communicating their thought process. A simple way to address that is to use an answer-first approach. Say you are trying to explain how Uber will become profitable.... You can come up with a long speech on this and lose your audience or express yourself in a couple of sentences, gauge whether you have been able to land your point and then dive deep into the nuances.

Essentially, logic is a fixable problem if we are prepared to spend time thinking through our line of argument and explain it clearly.

3. *Empathy:* Empathy is important. We know that. It is also in vogue. These days tyrants and dictators freely throw around the E word but it doesn't quite work. Why is that? Empathy of convenience is worse than no empathy at all. Pretending to care for someone or some community doesn't work beyond a certain point.

The key aspect to keep in mind is that if any of the three aforementioned variables wobble, the entire edifice of trust falls apart—both at a personal and organizational level.

SUCCESS GPS

Ask yourself four questions—what are you, where do you come from, where are you going and when will you get there. Write your answers down and keep repeating this exercise every month.

Remember that your current self will always make you feel that you have a lot more to do and that is great as a motivational tool (assuming you get motivated that way). However, if you want to know how you performed or in other words figure out if you are successful, refer to your past aspirations. Do this consistently and you will know where you stand.

MOTIVATION MATRIX

An author, Daniel Pink, offers a three-pronged approach that can help us navigate the passion/motivation challenge. With the help of scientific research in the labs of MIT and practical advice gleaned from being someone who got into a prestigious law school (Yale Law School) but didn't practice law for a day, Pink suggests that unless we have the combination of autonomy, mastery and purpose, we will continue to be unmotivated. And if we are not motivated, our passion will either misguide us or fade away. Both can be disastrous.

With this in mind, let us dive deep into Pink's framework.

The first factor of the three-pronged approach is autonomy. It is our innate desire to be self-directed but the extent of autonomy depends upon the kind of person we are. Some of us thrive in anarchy and some need direction to function. Thinking about where you stand on the spectrum is critical. There is a reason why some terrific entrepreneurs are terrible employees and vice versa.

The second is mastery. We often make the mistake of confusing passion with purpose. While purpose is focused on discovering meaning for self and society, passion may turn out to be an inward-looking whim.

Passion is a by-product of focused work. Real estate investor and Shark Tank's 'Shark', Barbara Corcoran, is often heard saying that she didn't follow her passion. She stumbled on it as she was working relentlessly to solve a problem she cared about. Research done by the likes of Oxford University's William MacAskill and the author, Cal Newport, provides that engaging work helps us develop passion, not the other way around.

The third and last factor is purpose. We all want our work to contribute to something larger than us. Voltaire was right when he said that work spares us from three evils: boredom, vice and need but he didn't live in the age of AI. In the digital era, if work doesn't add meaning to our lives, it will cease to exist.

UNPEELING LAYERS OF ANXIETY

Anxiety, both professional and otherwise, manifests itself in multiple ways. There is an obvious symptom and a not so obvious cause. We are trained to articulate what we are going through but unpeeling why we are going through it can be challenging.

Let's understand it with an example. Suppose you are going through a rough patch at work. The symptoms could include you lashing out at your friends/partner, sweating before the weekly status calls and a general feeling of hopelessness where you struggle to visualize a better future.

Many of us try to treat the problem by managing the symptoms. It never works. At best, it serves as a temporary distraction.

To mitigate anxiety, you need to be intimate with it. I don't want to give you platitudes like 'face your fear' or inflict a motivation quote on you but I do want you to visualize the scenario that you most dread and figure out what triggers it. This is obviously easier said than done, but surely worth a try.

It turns out that habits and triggers repeat themselves. They follow predictable patterns. If we catalogue them or just make a note, we will be a step closer to knowing what's truly making us sweat. By being intimate with anxiety, we tend to articulate it with our support system much better, thereby taking actionable steps towards beating it.

MEASURING YOUR IMPACT: THE NON-CV VERSION

If you just add up the impact of work people claim to have done on their CVs, almost all global challenges would be solved today. So where is the disconnect?

There are several challenges to quantifying your impact both on your CV and your inner-self.

Let's explore them these challenges:

1. Many times the work you do is hard to quantify. You are obliquely impacting something which in turn might move the needle somewhere someday. Hard to figure out, isn't it?

2. We are conditioned, especially in emerging economies, to show that we are working very hard. That is why many CVs tend to focus far more on input than on output. It comes as no

surprise that most CVs, at least in the first few drafts I read, sound a lot like JDs (job descriptions).

3. The quantification puzzle: I agree that honest quantification of your work is hard. To counter the challenge, many people go to the other extreme: They take quantum leaps of faith to enunciate their impact.

The real challenge is the non-CV impact. This is the impact you have on your inner-self. Do you know the difference between self-respect and narcissism?

Self-respect is the reputation you have of your own self. You can't have secrets with yourself.

Narcissism is the shame-based fear of being ordinary.

Many ambitious students and professionals grapple with both self-respect and narcissism. Sometimes we try and counter the self-respect challenge by becoming narcissistic.

It obviously backfires. So how might we measure our impact after all? Nothing seems to work.

I believe it all begins with thinking big and acting small. Big, hairy goals are accomplished with a consistent set of small actions that compound. We should measure our impact by first breaking the big goal into smaller parts and then measuring the impact of our smaller actions over a period of time. Every action has some impact. We need to train ourselves to figure out how we lived up to the micro goal.

In addition, we don't need to get lost in micro-details. Once we are consistent with our small actions, we are able to visualize the larger output.

Do you want to solve the education crisis? The answer is to start by figuring out how you might make five students ready for their future.

Do you want to scale your company? The answer is to not get distracted by funding shenanigans. Great companies are built on strong customer insights. Get to know the unarticulated needs of your users.

Consistency gives confidence, and confidence empowers us to take risks and absorb shocks that are sure to come our way.

In a world where everyone claims to be achieving so much, you should take a break and focus on what small action you can take to build a world you want to live in. If you are already doing so, great. If not, you might want to start today and measure what matters to you and not to your neighbour or posts on your social media wall.

COMPETITION IS FOR LOSERS

In *Zero to One*, Peter Thiel explains that the ultimate goal of a company is to become a creative monopoly. Quoting Leo Tolstoy's *Anna Karenina* and contextualizing it in a business setting, Theil states that all happy customers are different. Each one earns a monopoly by solving a unique problem. All failed companies are the same: They failed to escape competition. Basically, the more we compete, the less we gain. Future unicorns should try and explore synergies. Competing with each other on similar value propositions and tweaking on fringes is unlikely to work.

This is true for both companies and people. We are wrongly taught all through our years in school and college that winning the race or competition will set us on the path towards long-term success. Having interviewed thousands of successful people all around the world, I can assure you that most of them succeeded not because they competed. They succeeded because they chose carefully.

When you are competing hard with someone you are indirectly admitting that with a little more luck, a little more effort and a little better strategy, they can win. Simply put, you are beatable. What is it that you can do so well that competing with you isn't something that most people will look forward to? What are you uniquely suited to do? Where will the impact/input ratio be highest?

POWER OF ENDINGS

Endings matter, much more than we realize or give credit to. It turns out that Nobel Laureate Daniel Kahneman has an explanation for this. He calls it the 'duration neglect' where we often tend to downplay how long an episode lasts and magnify what happens at the end.

This encoding power of endings morphs many of our opinions and subsequent decisions. Several scientific studies show that we often evaluate movies, vacations and even dates not by the full experience but by certain moments, especially towards the end. Science tells us that when we rate our Uber/Ola/DiDi driver or provide feedback to our Airbnb host, much of our final evaluation is our reaction to the conclusion.

Moving beyond dates and cab rides, let us explore political elections —the cornerstone of democracies. When asked, most voters say that their decision is based on the performance evaluation of the full term but researchers tell us that that is categorically untrue. In fact, many studies have shown that voters decide who to vote for based on the election year economy—the culmination of a four out of five years sequence, not the entire duration. This 'end heuristic', political scientists like Berkeley's Gabriel Lenz argue, leads to 'myopic voting' and eventually 'myopic policies'.

Many believe that Hillary Clinton would probably be the American president had FBI's Director, James Comey, not sent a letter to Congress on 28 October 2016. The letter was shared 10 days before the election and stated that the FBI had learned of the existence of emails that appear to be pertinent to the investigation into the private email server that Clinton used as Secretary of State, upended the news cycle and soon halved Clinton's lead in the polls, imperilling her position in the electoral college.

Without getting sucked into a political debate, let us get back to the core issue, that is, endings. Julie Brines and Brian Serafini concluded that even heartbreaks and divorces are not immune to timing. They follow a distinct seasonal rhythm. Divorce filings spike in the months of March and August. The duo speculates that the twin peaks may be influenced by domestic rituals and family calendars. A Bloomberg reportage suggests that divorce attorneys have a high season in January and February, when holidays are over and people can finally stop pretending to be happy. Over the winter holidays, spouses give the marriage one last try before knocking the doors of lawyers. Contentious divorces require 4–6 weeks of preparation—this explains the March outburst. The same thing happens at the end of the school year. Parents keep it together till May and head to the lawyer by June/July, explaining the spike in August. Thankfully, I have no hands-on experience with divorce and have relied on Daniel Pink's analysis.

Endings help us encode and evaluate but they also twist our memory, cloud our judgement and alter our perception by overweighing final moments and neglecting the totality.

No research or scientific analysis can take away the pain of endings. That's why we have literature and art that nudge us into new beginnings. After all, every story is a happy story if we know where to put an end to it.

Conclusion

Magic happens at intersections, like when we combine math and music, physics and poetry, technology and empathy. I have always searched for such intersections and come to the conclusion that the first step towards meaningful change is to realize that cheerful cooperation and collaboration are far more potent than cut-throat competition—the violent buzzword of the day. Empowering others is the shortest and the most meaningful route to self-empowerment.

Meaningful and meaningless are Siamese twins. Choosing purpose over futility needs deliberate practice, community engagement and most importantly figuring out a unique way to add specific value to others. Through the case studies, mental models, philosophies and research presented in the book, I hope you are able to enjoy the adventure of learning, unlearning and building a career that makes a meaningful difference.

About the Author

Utkarsh Amitabh is the founder of Network Capital (network capital.tv), one of the world's largest career intelligence communities, Chevening Fellow at Oxford University and a World Economic Forum Global Shaper, who represented the community at the Annual Meeting in Davos. Set up with the core belief that everyone has something to learn and something to share, Network Capital has organically grown to become a global tribe of 100,000+ mentors from 104 countries, and content created by the community has been published by Harvard Business School, Harvard Business Review, *Mint* and *The Economic Times*.

Being passionate about public–private partnerships, Utkarsh shaped Network Capital's partnership with Government of India's Atal Innovation Mission to build India's largest mentoring program.

Utkarsh graduated with an MBA from INSEAD Business School where he was recognized as the Andy Burgess Scholar for Social Entrepreneurship. He is a Chevening Fellow at Oxford University and the torchbearer of Ashoka University's Young India Fellowship.

His work experience includes working with Microsoft, Harley-Davidson Motor Company and Teach for India. He is passionate about using technology to match talent and opportunities, and was part of the team from Microsoft that helped build India's first smart village, which is now recognized in the Prime Minister's book of pioneering innovations.

Utkarsh has a weekly column focused on future of work with *Mint*, one of India's largest business newspapers with an online reach of

33 million readers. His articles have been published by the World Economic Forum, *Indian Express, The Economic Times, The Times of India* and *Scroll.*

He has been selected among the 20 most distinguished Indian professionals by international media outlet, Quartz. The 'Quartz Pros' list includes Padma Vibhushan winners like Kris Gopalakrishnan, and Anand Mahindra, the Chairman of the USD 21 billion conglomerate, Mahindra Group.

Last year Utkarsh was awarded two fellowships for distinguished achievement: Raisina Young Fellowship by Observer Research Foundation and the INK Fellowship for being among the top 20 young achievers around the world who are both making a difference at work and in society.

Utkarsh has delivered speeches and participated in panel discussions on the need to democratize career intelligence and inspiration at Davos, Harvard, INSEAD, University of Michigan, IIT, IIM, etc. He regularly appears on television shows to share his views about how technology is changing career principles. His networkcapital.tv podcast has been downloaded more than 100,000 times.

Printed in Great Britain
by Amazon